MW01242164

GOAL-SETTING

HABITS TO ACHIEVE YOUR GOALS AND SUCCEED IN THE LIFE YOU WANT

Nathan Bynum

Edited by

Adalyn Vaughan

Elizabeth Bynum

Bill Bynum

Sam Bynum

Get the FREE Goal-Setting Templates to complement the skills learned in this book at:

reachfuelpotential.com

DEDICATION

By retaining a young learner's nonpartisan nature and combining it with the discernment of an experienced elder, we will never stop improving. This book is written with that person in mind. When you help yourself, you increase your ability to help others in turn. Put your oxygen mask on first. Otherwise, you can't save anyone. Leave everyone better than when you found them. I hope when you read this, you feel that I have done that for you.

Table of Contents

WHY I WROTE THIS BOOK

I have always enjoyed learning and improving myself in every aspect of life. Because I have been interested in learning so many different subjects and achieving several goals I set for myself, I have made it my mission to discover ways to learn and achieve goals more efficiently. From this, I have crafted a universal process to succeed in any endeavor. Much of this learning has come through various books, podcasts, Ted Talks, and mentors in my life. I know that time is the one thing that we will never get back. Because I value the lives of others and want the best for everyone, I want them to be able to make the most of their time. I want them to achieve whatever goals they have in mind and waste as little time as possible to reach their full potential. My goal is to make that achievable for you by providing you with the best information in a concise, no-fluff manner; I will not waste your time so that you will be able to spend more of it obtaining the life of your dreams.

According to a study done by Scranton University, only 8% of people who set goals achieve them. My goal is to raise that number. I want to free people from the constant frustration of not getting what they're aiming for. I am doing that through this book and a video course that is in the works. These both aim to answer specific questions you may have about how to achieve any goal you desire. I am also building a community of people united with the desire to create the life they want, one goal at a time. This community will help create accountability. The lack of accountability is a widespread factor of failure in completing our goals.

WHY YOU MAY BE HESITANT TO READ THIS BOOK

People sometimes stray from the idea of goal setting because it's cliché. Saying it's cliché has even become cliché. But the fact of the matter is, there are so many incomplete systems that are too vague and hard to follow, made by people who have not done the research, tested it, proved it, and compiled it all into one single place. People get bits and pieces of advice, try it, and become discouraged. They face obstacles that they didn't prepare for after just being told to make "S.M.A.R.T." goals. Inadequate goal-setting systems put a bad taste in people's mouths about the whole idea of goals. That is why I am passionate about giving people a system that actually works for them and yields the results they want. We are wired to achieve goals. We are teleological organisms that only need a complete and realistic process to achieve our goals efficiently.

CHAPTER 1: YOU ARE THE ARCHITECT

Where Did our Childhood Dreams Go?

Why is it that when we are young, we can dream so passionately and have such specific ideas in mind about what we want to be, have, and accomplish? Then, we grow up and believe that our dreams were impossible. One might answer that question by saying, "we don't understand the intricacies of what we imagine as a child," or "we don't know all the challenges we will face while trying to achieve our goal." But who is it that puts these limitations on us? Who tells us we don't have what it takes to get what we were once so passionate about?

The collective views of society can get into our heads and discourage us from believing in ourselves. The story of the first 4-minute mile is powerful. It wasn't until 1954 that it finally happened, although, as explained in John Bryant's book, runners had been vigorously striving for a sub-4-minute mile since 1886. After years of failure, Bryant writes, "It had become as much a psychological barrier as a physical one. And like an unconquerable mountain, the closer it was approached, the more daunting it seemed."[1] Many doctors in the early 20th century believed it was physiologically impossible. When Banister finally broke the 4-minute mark, everyone saw that it was possible, and other runners began to break it as well. It is dangerous to determine your limits based on what society deems as impossible.

The only person on this earth that has the ultimate power over what we do is ourselves. But, just understanding that isn't enough. The reason we don't believe in ourselves is that our goal may seem too far out of reach and unrealistic. We may have already tried to chase our dreams but to no avail. If any of this resonates with you, then that's okay. Chasing dreams is not what we should do; it is too unpredictable and unreliable. We need a structured system to build upon and get concrete repeatable results.

The Marquee

I have come up with an analogy that I will be referring to throughout this book. One reason I have done so is because it creates a natural structure that will easily flow. But more importantly, the memories we have are formed by connections. Therefore, the following information that you will read will stick with you much more quickly and permanently because you will have a corresponding picture to go with it. Mattias Ribbing, one of the few people ever to achieve the title Grand Master of Memory, advises people reading nonfiction books to pick one picture per concept to visualize to increase their comprehension and retention dramatically. Through this continuous analogy, you will already have built-in images to keep in your mind while reading the various concepts. The visual I will be using is a Marquee (large circus tent).

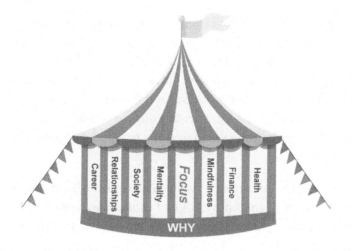

We start with the idea of the finished structure (the goal). But at this point, we don't know how to get there. This is where a blueprint (the how) comes in. The blueprint takes a concept and breaks it down into feasible steps and components to show us what materials we need and in what dimensions. Many times, we will have an idea of something we want to do like "play guitar" or "learn Spanish" or "learn coding" but not initially know the reason why.

Without knowing our why, we will soon lose our momentum because we won't have the motivation in our minds that we need. Our "why" is our foundation (the steel ground bars connecting the pillar poles). Next comes our support pillars. These are the 7 facets of our life that will be affected to some degree regardless of what goal we decide to pursue. The 7 facets include career, finance, health, mentality, mindfulness, relationships, and society. The pillars are all built up by different habits that we have (the links that make up the pole). The more habits we have in place, the more potential we have to reach our desired goal. In the middle of our Marquee, we have our center mast pole. This pole represents the focus we need to get to the top. The canopy goes on top, and thus we have reached our goal. It is the same Marquee that we envisioned from the beginning. Simple, right? Don't worry. Throughout the book, we will go into detail to explain the various steps to build our own personal Marquee.

You are the architect of your future. Today's architects have learned from the knowledge of those who have come before them and use it to build up their own dreams. As an architect, your blueprint will guide you through the construction process. Without a clear goal in mind, you will just wander aimlessly.

Through the construction process and evaluation of your goals and pillars, it will start to become more apparent what is essential to you in life.

CHAPTER 2: AVOID THE COMMON PITFALLS

View everything in a good light, and the path you need to take will become much clearer. Where others see obstacles, you will see challenges that will allow you to grow. Your energy will be focused in the right place, and you will begin seeing solutions in your life.

Common Reasons People Don't Reach Their Goals

- Self-doubt
- Losing motivation
- Going after too many goals at once
- Not knowing what goal to go for
- Not setting mini-goals
- Unclear picture of exactly what the goal looks like
- Allowing distractions to steal our focus
- Lack of helpful habits
- Unwilling to put off a small amount of instant gratification for a massive amount of sustaining gratification
- Not enough time
- Negativity
- Justification
- Excuses
- Rationalization

- Perception
- Blame shift

    Some people don't care to change or improve. They are fine being stagnant in an unproductive routine. The danger of this is that the world is ever-changing. When their world gets rocked, they aren't prepared to adapt with it. They know something needs to change, but they don't know how to make it happen. They haven't spent time thinking about what they want and setting goals to challenge themselves to grow. Sometimes it takes our world being rocked for us to realize this. Maybe that is you. The good news is that you are already ahead and gaining momentum by reading this book and learning how to do something about it. Don't stop there; apply what you learn to your life. Never stop pushing yourself to learn and develop your ability to set and achieve goals. In time, you will have the life you've always wanted.

    We will cover all of these topics throughout the rest of the book and specifically address the techniques for combatting each situation. We will approach these problems in a solution-based fashion. Successful people focus on what they want and the solutions on how to get there. Unsuccessful people focus more on the problems that they currently have in life. They feel overwhelmed, stressed, and tired because they are allocating so much energy to these obstacles. On the other hand, successful people focus on accomplishing what they want, work hard, and are refreshed by the continual progress.

Regret

Many of us have had a goal in the past that, for one reason or another, we didn't follow through with, and wound up feeling regret for. Maybe it seemed like too much work, or we had distractions in our lives holding us back. Perhaps we knew it was something beneficial but didn't give much thought to all the benefits we would receive. We didn't want to devote more time to it, and it wasn't until later we looked back on it and saw how great it could have been. I have had all of these thoughts, and sometimes I do feel regret. However, it is an unproductive mindset to get bogged down by what we can't control now. It could be that we can make an action plan to see that old goal through today. But sometimes it is too late.

In this case, you can utilize the frustration that it can create in your mind to have missed an opportunity to achieve something great. You can use that frustration as motivation to keep you going on the pursuits you now have in mind and let go of the past. Let your regret fuel you, not foil you.

It's uncomfortable not to have closure in our endeavors, and we will be utilizing the flip side of that coin to our advantage later on when we are setting our mini-goals to build our motivation. But keep in mind that negativity does more harm than good. It slows us down and leads us to make excuses. Remember that life is the sum of millions of individual moments. The only moment that matters now is the moment we are living in, and what we decide to do with that moment will shape all the ones that we will have in the future.

Eliminate Self-Doubt

The very fact that you are reading this book means that you care about improving your life. If we are improving ourselves, then that means the best version of ourselves lies in the future. But if we continuously doubt our abilities, we aren't going to get very far. There are different reasons for this fear that we will discuss and find solutions for. In scientific research performed by Thomas Gilovich (Cornell University), Victoria Medvec (Northwestern University), and Kenneth Savitsky (Williams College), it was discovered that a major cause of self-doubt is due to our natural tendency to be absorbed in how we feel and what we are thinking.[1] We then project these feelings onto our perception of how others view us and assume they are wrapped up in thinking about us as much as we do. But the truth is, other people are generally too busy thinking about how they feel or what they believe, not constantly scrutinizing any tiny mistake we may be making. So, our insecurity is built from our misconception that all the people around us are judging our flaws. Sometimes they do, but anyone who is trying to tear us down isn't worth our time. We simply need to focus on our own opinions and understanding of ourselves and not expend our energy on worrying what we think others think of us. Once we realize this, we will have much more energy to focus on taking actionable steps to get what we want out of life.

We are capable of so much more than we give ourselves credit for. If we simply let go of the unhealthy and untrue labels that we give ourselves, we will be free of our self-inflicted jails. You are responsible for what happens to you. Own that responsibility yourself. Be free and take that next step to change your life.

Fears and Adversity

List out the fears you have about working on your goal. How do having these fears hurt you? How do having these fears and allowing them to dictate your actions hold you back? Now, how would your life be improved if you didn't have these fears? Fears are restraints that, if we allow them to, can hinder important aspects of our lives. We need to examine our fears in an objective manner and see them for what they truly are. When we do this, we can make our decisions rationally and do what we need to do.

We don't live in a perfect world, and thus, obstacles will arise. This is a fact of life, but it is not meant to discourage us. We have dealt with obstacles throughout our lives. When everything is going well, it is harder for us to see a need to improve. We have a danger of being stagnant and not growing. There is a vast difference between being content and being stagnant. Being content is about seeing the blessings we have in our lives and being grateful for them.

Being stagnant is not working towards a better future with the talents that we have. We can be content and still recognize that we are not perfect and continue to sharpen our skills, such as working on our relationships, giving more to others, etc. Adversity has the benefit of making this clearer for us and revealing an area we need to work on. It calls us to ACTION. As Herodotus put it, "Adversity has the effect of drawing out strength and qualities of a man that would have lain dormant in its absence."[2] Either we can look at adversity with disdain, or we can see it as an opportunity. Only good can come from choosing the latter.

"Limitations inspire creation."[3] -Charles Bello

The Funny Reality

There's a funny reality connected to people being content with the status quo. Some people simply don't like change and would love for things to stay just how they are, and for them, they probably will stay that way for a time. These people allocate their energy to keeping things that way and don't seek new opportunities. Like the story of the one talent man in the book of Matthew, they bury their talents in hopes of keeping it safe. They long for security and believe they'll have it by "laying low." Unfortunately for them, as we discussed earlier, things change. This is the only certainty in life. If we aren't prepared to change, we get swept away in the chaos of this world. We need to be able to predict, adapt, and continuously be moving forward towards making ourselves better, making the world more joyful, making our society a better place to live, and investing in ourselves and generations who are to come. The future is full of uncertainties, but things will certainly be better if we continue to move forward. "The more you seek security, the less of it you have. But the more you seek opportunity, the more likely it is that you will achieve the security that you desire." -Brian Tracy

Time

You may have heard of ROI (Return on Investment). ROI is an essential concept in financial planning. Money is a necessary commodity for functioning that we will talk about under the 7 facets, but it is also something you can always make more of (more on that later). ROTI (Return on Time invested) is a pressing concept to learn now. The time you spend on setting your goals will save you a significant amount of time in the future, and unlike money, you are given a finite amount.

Here are some of the most common reasons people believe they do not have enough time.

- Indecisiveness

- Having no boundaries on their time

- Social media

- Television or Netflix bingeing

- Time with people who don't have their best interest

- Work-life imbalance

Before you even start making the blueprint for your goal, you need to consider the fact that time is our most valuable commodity, so we must be minimalistic with our goals and decide which goal is worth pursuing. The newest way of thinking about time management is discussed in Rory Vaden's book *Procrastinate on Purpose*.[4] A significant point of the book is one that I will apply how you choose your goal. The idea is that we have a list of things we want to get done, and we only have 24 hours in the day to do them, so how do we choose which one to do first? I will give a simplified example of this to demonstrate the idea. Two things that I wanted to accomplish were to write a book and learn how to type. Writing a book and being able to express all the knowledge I was accumulating from books, interviews, and other sources seemed much more important and fulfilling. But since I needed to accomplish both goals anyways, I decided it made more sense to invest my time wisely and learn to type before writing this book. I achieved both goals and saved an incredible amount of time doing one before the other. This example may not apply to you because you probably learned how to type as a 7-year-old, but the same principle applies to whatever you may want to achieve.

Sometimes choosing the right step will prevent a potential problem and, therefore, save you time. In my interview with Charles Stephenson, current City Manager of Temple Terrace, Florida, and former owner of a construction company, he talked to me about his time as a business owner.

"When I was in the construction business, in the morning, I was shoveling mud out of the gutter. There's a reason I did that because I didn't want another complicated matter down the road because all that mud that's in the gutter is going to end up in the storm system, and then I have to fix the storm system. My goal in the morning was to get the mud out of the gutter. But my goal in the afternoon was to get out of the mud, put a suit on, and go down and borrow millions of dollars for a project. That's the goal. Now at the end of the day, when I woke up in the morning, I had 2 goals, get the mud out of the gutter and get a bunch of money to build a project and if you set those goals, you will achieve those goals, you will get them. If I woke up in the morning and said: 'What am I going to have to do today? Well, maybe I think I'll go downtown and try to get some money' that's going to get sidetracked. 'I think I need to clean the gutters' that's going to get sidetracked. You need to wake up in the morning and say, 'this is what I'm going to get done today.'"

Having a grasp on the big picture gives us the foresight to predict potential obstacles that may arise if we don't pick the right short-term goals first. As a business owner, there were many tasks Charles could have picked first that would seem more glamorous or feel more rewarding in the moment than cleaning the mud from the gutters. However, he prioritized his tasks based on what would save time and money in the long run, which is precisely what we need to do.

"Establishing a priority on goals is one of those things that you have to look at the whole big picture." -Charles Stephenson

Chapter 3: Choosing Your Goal

Maybe you don't already have a goal in mind, but you know you want more out of life, or you want to live and experience life more fully. Maybe you just don't want to be stagnant. Whether you have a goal yet or not, remember to base your next step on your own value system instead of on what is popular. Vividly imagine your life in 5 years from now, your ideal self, what does it look like? What do you feel and see around you? Where are you working or not working anymore? What skills do you have? The future has no limits. We do not know all the events that will unfold in our lives in the future or what resources will be available to us then. Therefore, do not place limitations on what you want to achieve based on your present circumstances.

When I asked Charles Stephenson how he chooses his goals, he replied, "You have to understand the big picture." He then explained how he must take into account the good of everyone in the city to choose his goals. When he thinks of or is presented with a major idea he wants to pursue, he will write it down, set it on his desk, then come back to it twice to let himself look at it with a fresh set of eyes each time. On the third time, if he still thinks it is worthy of pursuing, he will go for it.

How do you see the big picture in your life? The more clearly you can see it, the more accurate your next step will be. To find it, ask yourself the following questions.

1. What is different in my ideal life 5 years from now than in my current life?
2. What do I see when I visualize my ideal future that gives me the most joy?
3. Are there any prerequisite goals that I should accomplish before achieving the goal I want the most to take control of and save my valuable time?

After taking careful consideration of these questions, you should now have your goal.

Just Start

The one thing that guarantees that you won't get anywhere is simply not starting. Starting something is not a guarantee that you will finish it, but it does guarantee that you will be closer to your goal than before. If you start building on your goal, you will learn what works for you or certain things not to do, but either way, you will learn. You can't turn a car if you don't start it.

There are, as always, different excuses people make for not starting. Some people put off starting towards their goals because they want everything to be perfectly set in place before they do so. They may spend hours researching articles or videos on a subject, learning different techniques about what they want to do. They may study for hours on the perfect tools for the job. All of these tasks do have their place but only to a certain degree. Everything needs balance. Once initial research has been done, there is great value to just starting the actual process to get a feel for it. Reading and watching videos on a subject will never adequately prepare you for how something is going to feel. Once you've started the actual process, the material you take in after that will become much more meaningful to your understanding. Getting started will also undoubtedly raise questions you didn't realize you had before, and questions you generate will engage your mind intensely in the learning process.

"You miss 100% of the shots you don't take."[1] -Wayne Gretzky

This is going to sound extremely easy, but there is a very simple yet powerful technique to use when you feel frozen in place and don't want to start. Mel Robbins describes this technique in her book "The 5 Second Rule".[2] Our minds have been wired all of our lives to be triggered by countdowns; the alarms we have going off, school bells triggering us to leave class, a whistle blowing triggering us to start a play. We can take advantage of this hard wiring of our brains when we want to start something ourselves. When you have something that you know you need to do but don't feel your feet moving, just count down in your head, 5, 4, 3, 2, 1, Go. Don't think, just go. When I first heard about this technique, I was skeptical because of its simplicity. However, I tried it anyway, and it works surprisingly well. Sometimes "simple" can be overlooked, and a lot of times, it's just what we need.

Using Strategy as an Excuse

Trying to accomplish a massive feat without a plan is likely to end in failure. A well laid out plan will guide you along the way to reach your final destination. However, some people don't start because they want to have the perfect strategy in place before they start. There is no such thing as a perfect strategy because we cannot see into the future. You need to have adaptability built into your system. The real-world strategy is an ongoing, ever-adapting series of events.

Chapter 4: How to Accomplish it (The Blueprint)

Mind Map

A mind map is a visual way of displaying your thoughts. The main idea goes in the middle of the piece of paper with a circle around it. From that, a line is drawn outward, and at the end of that line, the next idea is written and circled. This continues until the ideas are all on the page.

Start with the goal in the center of your mind map and let the ideas flow. There are some universal techniques that we can use with any goal we are striving for, giving us a systematic way to reach it. A highly successful Czech businessman Honza Novak explained to me how he uses mind maps for all of his projects. He uses them to keep track of all the moving parts and ideas that go into designing and running a business. All goals have their own little intricacies. These intricacies are where mind mapping becomes your best friend. It gives you the freedom to be creative with problem-solving and solution-finding in a way that will make the connections evident, that other methods of brainstorming do not come close to. The way mind maps work will display the relationship of thoughts much clearer to you than a simple list, and you can easily add links to ideas anywhere you see fit later. Another reason these are great for this process is that when the ideas are flowing fast, you can write down a word or two to represent the key concepts, draw a line and-boom, you keep going—no need for full long sentences for everything to make sense.

Get a piece of paper or a mind mapping app and write your goal in the middle. Draw a bubble around it. Draw a line extending from your goal bubble for each of your main concepts. These are "resources," "steps," "analysis," "obstacles," and "why." Draw a bubble around each of these words. Draw another line for each of the ideas you have related to the specified bubbles.

• Resources. The resources section includes physical resources that you will need to complete your goal, as well as nonphysical resources. It is a broad area that will consist of any of the 7 facets of your life that may be beneficial to you completing this goal. It will also include traits you have, such as energy. If a 20-year-old wants to start a business, determining their resources may be discouraging at first blush. Finances may be the first one that comes to mind, and, likely, a 20-year-old does not have many financial resources compared to a 40-year-old. However, we all have our strengths. The typical 20-year-old will have much more

29

energy than a 40-year-old. This energy is a valuable resource they can leverage to their advantage. The 40-year-old will be wiser, have more experience, and, most likely, more money to utilize.

• Steps: List the steps you will be taking throughout the process. These are the mini-goals that you will be achieving. We will go into these in much more detail later.

• SWOT: Strengths, Weaknesses, Opportunities, and Threats- List strengths that you have that will facilitate this process. Write down potential weaknesses in this area. These are skills or abilities that you can either improve on or outsource. Write any opportunities you can think of that give you an edge with this project. Lastly, write any possible threats to the completion of the goal.

• Obstacles and Solutions: Write down any potential obstacles you can think of that may hinder you from working on or reaching your goal. Linked off of the "obstacles," write down all of the solutions you come up with to prevent these obstacles from winning.

• Why: The more passionate you are about something, the more likely you are to finish it. Knowing why you are passionate about it and having that in front of you will keep you motivated.

• Sources: Sources come from a plethora of places. These include websites, videos, books, articles, experts, courses, or anything at your disposal to facilitate the learning process.

- Ideas: Whatever comes to your mind about this topic that is not covered under one of the main categories goes here. You can also branch off and make your own customized categories to fit your needs.

Visualizing the Goal (Final Marquee)

We are very visual creatures. This is apparent by much of the terminology we use from day-to-day. If you couldn't visualize what I meant, do you SEE what I'm talking about now? Why do we appreciate walking around a prominent building in which you can't make a noise and stare at rectangles on the wall with paint on them? If that's not to your liking, why do we communicate now by taking a selfie on Snapchat and sometimes adding some words to it instead of just texting or calling someone? I think those two examples cover the preferences of the major demographics. Vision is part of who we are, and we need a vision to accomplish something extraordinary, or we just wander aimlessly. Michael Angelo said about one of his most famous pieces, "I saw the angel in the marble and carved until I set him free."[1] Once you have a clear image in your head of what you are working towards, the steps to get there will become apparent. But just like the marble piece Michelangelo created, it will still take work.

Leaders are visionaries. They have a clear vision of what the future needs to look like, make a plan on how to get there, and then take ACTION. Whether or not we are a manager, a coach, a parent, or a low-level employee, we still are leaders. We have led our own life in whatever direction we are going by the actions we take every day. Once we realize this, we will understand the importance of having a vision for our life. The paths of our life are like the ocean, and our vision is a lighthouse that we keep in sight to make sure our course is steady and the moves we are making are bringing us towards our goal.

According to a study published by María José Méndez, 90% of the information transmitted to our brains is visual information.[2]

Dr. Lynell Burmark, an expert in visual literacy, explains, "unless our words, concepts, ideas are hooked onto an image, they will go in one ear, sail through the brain, and go out the other ear. Words are processed by our short-term memory, where we can only retain about seven bits of information (plus or minus 2). Images, on the other hand, go directly into long-term memory where they are indelibly etched."[3]

Not only does the visualizing process affect the efficiency and clarity of our thinking, but visual images also evoke stronger emotions. This is because of the way our brain is structured. Our emotions are processed in the medial temporal region of our brain, which is the same place our visual memory is encoded.

One technique that memory masters use is to create a story out of the pieces of information they are trying to remember. Because they understand the influential role our emotions play in our cognition, they create highly emotional stories. The take away from this is that the more we visualize our goal and create images in our head for it, and the steps to get there, the more powerfully our emotions will guide us and keep us motivated on this entire journey.

Foundation-Why You Want to do This

Whatever your answers are to this question, you need to have a simple picture associated with them that you visualize in colorful 3D. Perform this visual exercise whenever you begin your scheduled work on your goal, and also any time you feel discouraged about reaching your goal.

Not all "why's" are created equal. We only have a strong foundation when the reason why we are doing something is in line with our passions and principles. When we achieve this congruency, we will be unstoppable. We overcome all obstacles because our passion is fueling us.

Specific

The image we have in our heads of what our end goal looks like needs to be extremely specific. One of the reasons for this is that if it isn't, then our planning process will be impossible since we don't know what we are building. Also, we need to be able to tell when we are done. Having a clear picture is essential because the satisfaction that comes from the dopamine release only comes when we know we have completed a goal. In order for this to happen, we need a clear picture of our complete goal.

Overview of OKRs and KPIs

If you have done much investigation in strategies behind goal setting, you have most likely encountered these two acronyms at some point. However, what exactly these acronyms entail or even the difference between them may still remain a mystery to you. In the strategies we will be using in this book, we will utilize some of the principles behind these two concepts. Consequently, I will briefly explain them.

Let's go back to our Marquee analogy. Our goal is, of course, what we have decided to be the outcome we will obtain. OKRs (Objective and Key Results) and KPIs (Key Performance Indicators) will be parts of our blueprint (how). The OKRs will be the ambitious mini-goals that will get us to our final one. They are objectives that we can measure numerically and are designed to push us forward towards our Marquee. KPIs are generally more about measuring the performance of a system that is already in place. We will have a much larger number of KPIs than OKRs. When we look at the KPIs, we will know if there is something that we need to correct.

Unless we are focused on growing a specific KPI, then it is likely that it will remain fairly constant. Where this may get confusing is that our KPI can also be our OKR, depending on what we want. Here is an example. Let's say we own a website, and our goal is to increase its revenue by 10% in 2 months. Up until this point, one of our KPIs has been the number of visitors to our website. We were happy with the number before because it was stable, and we had other objectives we were working on in other areas of our site. However, we know that the product we are producing is extremely beneficial to our customers, and the price we are selling it for is fair. So, to increase our revenue, we must reach more people. Our new goal now moves our old KPI (number of visitors) to one of our OKRs.

Deadlines

Deadlines have been part of our lives since our school years, and they don't go away. Unfortunately, it wasn't until my fourth year of college that I became proficient in this area. I'm embarrassed to say that, up until then, I was a major procrastinator. I justified this behavior by the fact that I'm much more creative, and my mind works much faster when I'm in a time crunch. When we are assigned a task, our brains automatically calculate how long it will take to complete it. If it is a large task, and we have five months until the deadline, our mind will tell us to procrastinate because it knows we have the capability of finishing it in 5 weeks if we work on it a few hours a day. But, as we approach the 5-week mark, the overconfidence bias comes in, and we decide we can finish it in 2 hard weeks.

However, in such a short period of time, our best work cannot be sustained for the necessary hours of work. We may get it done, but it will be far from our best work. Continuing the use of the school analogy, even if we make an A on a 2,500-word essay written the night before, that just shows the potential we had if we started on it much earlier. Still, I didn't want to lose the creative flow I would get into when I had a deadline. So, depending on the size of the project or paper, I started setting 4 or 5 incremental deadlines I would have to meet. I would treat these just like they were the real thing but break down the project, either in 1/4 or 1/5, depending on how many increments I set. Many goals will require much more time than this, but the same simple formula applies. When it gets to this point, we may become overwhelmed by how much time it looks like it is going to take us, but even if we only devote 30 minutes a day to our goal, that will carry us a long way. If this is the case, then ask yourself, "Is my goal worth 30 minutes a day?" When we frame it this way in our minds and see how little time we are going to be investing to reach our desired outcome, then it won't seem like too much to ask of ourselves. 30 minutes is only 2% of our day! If you did answer no, then the goal you have picked probably is not the right goal for you.

Number of Mini-Goals Equation

# of increments=Total estimated time to finish goal/ How long you will dedicate each day to reaching your goal

This equation allowed me to be much more productive and alleviated most of the real deadline's stress. It also gave me ample time to review my work, and if something unexpected came up the day it was due, it didn't create a crisis. The blueprint for our goals needs to work the same way. We must have a deadline for our final "Marquee," break down the construction job into allotted segments and plan incremental deadlines accordingly.

Whenever we complete a task, our brain releases dopamine. This feel-good hormone is another benefit of having these incremental deadlines set up for yourself. This release of dopamine will be associated with the goal you are striving to achieve, thus giving you more motivation to reach the end. The amount of dopamine released is based on the size of the task we have completed.

Setting the deadlines is a step that you will need to reevaluate each week, especially in the beginning, to adjust for how long tasks take compared to your estimation. Pick a specific day and time each week to devote to this.

As I mentioned earlier, one reason some will give up on their goals is because they underestimated the time or the amount of work necessary to reach it. When this occurs, we need to take a moment, see how far we have come from our starting point, enjoy the fact that we are getting better, and recognize we are that much closer to realizing our goal than we were before.

When You Will Work on it

You have your deadlines marked out on your calendar already, so you should have an idea of how much time this is going to take. Be deliberate about the time you mark out for the goal. Like all the other steps in this process, the more you work on your goals, the more accurate your time allotment skills will increase. Treat these appointments like doctors' appointments. You are free to schedule them whenever fits best. Once you have scheduled them, only change them if absolutely necessary.

Mini-goals

These mini-goals that we create give us a chance to reflect on what is working and adjust accordingly. When we do this, we become more efficient, decreasing our time wasted. For example, let's say we want to learn guitar, but we are a complete novice. We decide that we want to learn five songs on the guitar in one year. There are several mini-goals we will need to reach along the way to have gained this skill. I like to search the internet to find what is almost like a SparkNotes for learning a new skill. Type in "how long does it take to learn the steps of ___." I did this for guitar, and this is what I found from theguitarlesson.com:

"1-2 months: Play easy guitar songs (changing between and strumming of basic chords, single-string plucking songs with not much string jumping, chord arpeggios)

3-6 months: Play a bit more difficult songs, which require more technical elements. For example, songs requiring easier hammer-ons, pull-offs, and other easier lead guitar techniques.

1 year: Play intermediate level songs, including many very popular guitar songs, riffs, blues, and so on. You will probably start getting a more definitive feel for barre chords at around this time as well."[4]

Doing this quick research will give us an excellent target for a skill we know nothing about. We now need to pick a specific date that we believe we will reach each goal. This research doesn't tell us how long each day that we will need to practice, but that is something we will become better at estimating with time. We will now break down these goals into even smaller ones. More research is required to find out what chords we need to know for the five songs we want to learn. For example, what strumming pattern can we use universally in all of these songs? Once we have broken everything down into daily activities, we have completed the mini-goals step.

The mini-goals we have put into place will not only benefit us through marking our process and inducing creativity, but they also serve as the perfect place for reinforcing our behavior with small rewards. We can train our minds to enjoy the work we are putting in with the fundamental psychological rule of positive reinforcement. It doesn't have to be a huge reward as long as we put something in place.

CHAPTER 5: OTHER FACTORS FOR GOAL SUCCESS

Flow

Have you ever heard an interview with a pro athlete when they're describing being "in the zone"? Things seem to slow down, and their reaction time speeds up. They know precisely what they need to do, and it just seems to happen. The state of flow (being in the zone) can easily be seen in athletes, musicians, actors, or other professions that we can observe. It's more evident in them than others because they have so much practice being in the state of flow. Most likely, we have all experienced this in a task that we thoroughly enjoy and are challenged by, and in that moment, we are our most creative and productive selves. If videogames are your thing, you've probably felt it quite often. Videogame designers understand the addictive feeling of being in the zone and strategically design the games around this idea. The great thing is that once we learn the nine principles behind this state, we will be able to apply it to our professional life, personal interests, goals, or anything else we so choose.

The state of flow was popularized by Mihaly Csikszentmihalyi, a psychologist who has researched this idea for over 20 years. In his book, he paints a picture of flow in this way:

"Contrary to what we usually believe, moments like these, the best moments in our lives, are not the passive, receptive, relaxing time, although such experiences can also be enjoyable if we have worked hard to attain them. The best moments usually occur when a person's body or mind is stretched to its limits in a voluntary effort to accomplish something difficult and worthwhile. Optimal experience is thus something that we make happen. For a child, it could be placing with trembling fingers the last block on a tower she has built, higher than any she has built so far; for a swimmer, it could be trying to beat his own record; for a violinist, mastering an intricate musical passage. For each person, there are thousands of opportunities, challenges to expand ourselves."[1]

For this book's purposes, we can apply these principles to organizing our mini-goals to build towards our primary goal. Listed below are the 9 principles that, if we adopt, will systematically put us into flow.

Principle 1: Flow inducing goals- These are clear goals set that have a clear path, and you know when you have completed each task.

Principle 2: Effective feedback- Frequently evaluate where you are on the course to your goal so you can make corrections where needed. Clear mini-goals make this possible. The feedback also allows you to understand the overall map to your goal better and to see the future steps more clearly in your head.

Principle 3: Balance between current skills and challenge- This is where the idea of attainable goals comes in.

We need to set goals that will challenge us, but that we can still accomplish. Your mini-goals will start off easier at first, and you can increase the challenge as you improve and near your main goal.

Principle 4: Action and awareness merge- When the first three principles are aligned, this one will naturally follow. It gets easier after the first few mini-goals when you begin to become self-aware and competent in what you are doing. The structure behind goals will become second nature, and you will be able to focus more on what you are doing.

Principle 5: Distractions are excluded- As your action and awareness increase, your focus will follow and become much easier to obtain. The more you are aware of what you need to work on to achieve your goal, the more quickly you can recognize distractions and ignore them.

Principle 6: No worry about failure- Our perception changes everything. When we have these mini-goals in place, we learn more about ourselves and our current topic at every little step. If we don't get something done in the exact amount of time that we thought we would or do something wrong, it doesn't matter because we learned, and therefore, are better than when we started this journey.

Principle 7: Self-consciousness disappears- Worries about the past or the future disappear because we are so focused now on what we are doing in the present moment.

Principle 8: Time is distorted- People say time flies when you're having fun. This saying is incredibly accurate when it comes to flow. The scientific name for the state of flow is "transient hypofrontality." "Transient" indicates it is only for a certain amount of time. "Hypo" means under or less than what is typical. Finally, "frontality" is referring to the prefrontal cortex. When we are in flow, our prefrontal cortex, where our perception of time comes from, is temporarily resting.

Principle 9: Autotelic Activity- This means that you enjoy the journey to the goal. You enjoy getting better because you're getting closer to what you want. You know that the skills you are learning will also make you better in other areas. You may meet interesting people along the way. You get joy from bettering yourself.

When all of these principles are aligned, it is incredibly powerful for your success. They are all actionable principles that we can single out and develop to achieve flow in whatever activity we choose.

Finding the Proper Challenge Level

Flow will only occur when we find the proper level of challenge for our current skill level. Frustration, low self-efficacy, and a lack of motivation occur when we set goals that are too challenging for our skill level. Alternatively, when the challenge is too low, we will get bored and be much less productive and creative. When we find the proper balance, our productivity picks up, and we can focus on what we need to do.

Prerequisite Skills

Time is our most valuable asset, so we need to give a lot of thought to maximizing what we have. Just like in the example I gave of learning the skill of typing before writing this book, other goals may require skills that we don't even consider learning first because we want to start with what seems like the most important thing. Our first thoughts will be that we need to devote all our time to our primary goal, so we can't waste it on learning something else beforehand. However, we must consider the time we will save in the long run from spending a few hours learning a complimentary skill. I spent about 15 hours trying to break my old two-finger-typing habit and learning the most efficient way to type before starting to write. At first blush, it may have seemed more important to skip that because I would be 15 hours ahead on all the research and writing. However, throughout this whole process and the following books I will be writing, all the articles for my website, emails I will send, and everything else that will require typing, I will get my ROT back many times over.

Focus

Focus means having your awareness entirely in the present moment. Your awareness of the outside world disappears. The only thing left is what you need to do right now to accomplish your task. Your brain shuts off the unnecessary processes and uses its energy for only what is essential right now.

Focus may seem like a foreign concept in the world we live in with an ever-growing number of things begging us for attention, but this ability is one that will make or break our success in life. Now, more than ever, we need to invest our time in learning this skill and honing our ability until turning on our tunnel vision becomes second nature. There is a reason that racehorses have blinders on them. They keep one thing on their minds, the goal-the finish line, and everything falls into place. All of their preparation and hard work pays off. They get from point "a" to point "b" in the most efficient way possible. The jockeys achieve this by equipping each horse with blinders that only allow them to see the path right in front of their face. If our blinders temporarily slip and a distraction appears, the less time and energy we give to that distraction, the less our focus will waiver, and we can get back on track. Do not feed the monster.

The principles we discussed in flow make focus easily attainable. In addition to those, there are two vastly different ideas on how to achieve our ultimate state of focus. One is called the Pomodoro Technique[2], and the other is Deep Work.[3] They are nearly opposites of each other in their philosophies but let me suggest that they are both useful tools. A butcher knife is a handy tool, but you probably wouldn't be excited if your doctor was about to use that to cut you open for surgery instead of using a scalpel. You probably wouldn't be excited to be having surgery anyway, but you can see how they are both tools used for cutting flesh. However, there is a time and place for everything. Pomodoro is an excellent tool for getting tasks done that require less brainpower but are still necessary to get done. It helps with less exciting missions.

To use the Pomodoro Technique, hide all distractions, set a timer for 25 minutes, and work nonstop until it goes off. Once it goes off, stop wherever you are in your work. Don't worry about a stopping point because you will soon come back to it. You then set a timer for 5 minutes and can do whatever you want except for work on your project. Once that timer goes off, set a timer for 25 minutes, and repeat this work-and-relax cycle. Pomodoro is an effective technique for getting through monotonous work that does not require much deep thought. Deep work is a better choice for any task that requires deep thinking and creativity. We will discuss deep work in a later section.

Organization

In my interview with Kathy Williams of the Williams Fence Co. in Lakeland, Florida, the concept she kept referring back to was organization. Running a large, successful business means that there are a lot of moving parts. Staying organized keeps us on track and on schedule. The goal we pick will be made up of many smaller pieces that we will be working on in the times we choose. The fewer variables you have, the more you will realize which factor is the problem. It also helps us focus only on what is essential. An organized space and schedule will allow us to get more done in less time with less stress.

"Proper planning and preparation prevents poor performance."[4] -Stephen Keague

Willpower

A study done by the American Psychological association in 2011 showed that 27% of people said their lack of willpower was the most significant barrier to change.[5] Fortunately, this is a learnable skill. By setting up a system that we will want to follow, we naturally have much more momentum and action towards our desired outcome.

Working systematically will also allow us to predict possible obstacles we will face, whether external or internal, and will dramatically increase our odds of success. We are people with reasoning and prediction skills. We can make educated predictions based on how we know ourselves and our environments to be. However, we will not always get them right. Unpredicted obstacles, distractions, and emotions will arise, and it will be critical to our success that we persevere by using our willpower.

Like all of the topics discussed in this book, willpower is a skill, and a skill, by definition, is learnable. Every time we don't want to do something that we know we need to, and we do it anyway, we are training ourselves in this skill. Each time the neurons in our brain fire a signal between the synapses instructing a behavior, it wires the brain to repeat the same action more easily the next time.

Willpower is self-discipline in action. In addition to being a learnable skill, there are some tangible steps we can take to make sure it is easier to implement when needed. On a physiological level, willpower has an undeniable connection with our blood sugar levels and our sleep.[6] If we think back to a time that we didn't have much sleep the night before, perhaps even at this moment for some of you, we will begin to recall evidence of our brains inhibited performances. It's harder to remember information, and it's easier to get frustrated at the little things people do. Apply the above principles, and notice your willpower increase significantly.

Motivation

The three factors of motivation include the goals we set, emotions, and self-efficacy.

Once you have your vision in place and continue to focus on it, the results you will start seeing on the journey to your goal will help motivate you. This will become a cycle of positive results and continual motivation. The motivation will then perpetuate your progress to your goal. Also, as mentioned earlier, having a firm understanding of why we are working towards our goal is a picture that we will keep in our head to ensure that our motivation is at its highest.

Emotions have a massive impact on how motivated we feel. If we are worried about failure or are hostile towards our process, then our brains will expend much of its finite energy on these negative emotions. On the other hand, if we feel excited, curious, and a desire to contribute to the world, we will see our motivation increase significantly and remain that way.

Self-efficacy means that you believe in your ability to achieve your goals. Setting mini-goals that you know you can achieve will build your self-efficacy.

Minimalistic View of Goal-Setting

Eliminate anything that hinders you from reaching your goal. This means not only eliminating anything that directly affects the path but also eliminating anything that is a waste of your incredibly valuable time. Think back to the quote from Michelangelo about the marble angel. He envisioned what the end result needed to be, and from that vision, he could clearly identify what to get rid of to make his thoughts a reality.

"It's not the daily increase but daily decrease. Hack away at the unessential."[7] -Bruce Lee

Ockham's razor[8] parallels this philosophy. The premise of Ockham's razor is that when you have a set of choices, the simplest one is usually the best. It is a guideline to shave away the excess. The point of Ockham's philosophy is not laziness, but to remind us not to overcomplicate things with unnecessarily complex theories or potential solutions. "Things should be as simple as possible but not any simpler."[9] -Albert Einstein

The Joy of the Journey

The last principle of Flow (Principle 9) is that you need to realize what you are doing should be an autotelic activity. The ability to be in the present while also working towards a goal requires you to find joy in the journey. If you think you will only be happy after you achieve your goal, then you will have a hard life. There are times we need to push through activities that we don't enjoy if they are leading towards goals we believe will make us happy. But we may need to find a different goal if we don't experience any joy in the process. You will be thrilled once you achieve your goal, but you need to find joy now. If we believe we will only find happiness once we've reached our goal, we will likely become discouraged and lose motivation long before we get there. Chasing a particular outcome and lacking motivation is a recipe that leads some to cut corners or not produce quality. To alleviate either of these possibilities, we must be aware of why this happens and change our perspective on the necessary work to reach our goal. When we learn to enjoy the journey and find happiness in the process, we will keep our motivation.

In my interview with the talented singer-songwriter Charlie Imes, he explained the importance of the journey in this way.

"Enjoy the journey because the journey is really what it's all about. Wanting to get from point "a" to point "b", and getting to point "b" is great. Once you do that and you are reflecting back on it, it's like, 'Yes, it was great when I was able to play a stadium full of people,' so, that's the goal I want to play a big festival in front of a stadium full of people. Well, that's great. Once that happens, you can say, 'yes, those 2 hours that I got to do that were terrific, but you know, let me tell you about the journey and some of the things that happened along the way to get there,' because that's really where the fun is. Not that it wouldn't be fun to do the stadium, but really that's only lasting for 2 hours, and as great of a ride as that is, it's the journey to get you there. So, enjoy the ride."

Environment

A study conducted on office workers in London yielded surprising results. It showed that when we customize our environment, as little as adding a small memento or picture, it leads to an increase in productivity of up to 32%.[10] Too much clutter, however, monopolizes our mental bandwidth. This is because of all the excess stimulus our brain has to sort through.

Natural light is scientifically proven to boost our mood by lowering our cortisol levels and triggering the release of endorphins.[11] Sunlight is, of course, the optimal source, but incandescent light bulbs (if you can still find them) are the next best thing.

A study conducted by Exeter University proved the benefit of having plants in our work environment. The results showed a 15% increase in productivity and increased levels of concentration.[12]

Rest and Relax

A widely overlooked principle that is necessary for productivity is taking the time to relax. Many self-proclaimed gurus all over the internet promote a "hustle culture." This culture seems to be a backlash against all of the "get rich quick" scams. The "hustle gurus" try so hard to avoid this group that they vastly overcompensate. The lifestyle they primarily promote is unsustainable in the long run. There is a point of diminishing returns we will reach if we never take the time to rest and recharge. Radical ideas are advertised, and what is practical is not what is promoted. But the healthiest and most productive lifestyle is a balanced one.

Relaxation looks different for everyone. You may be most relaxed when you're in the middle of nature, listening to music, running, playing guitar, taking a walk, or something entirely different. What matters is that you find an activity that gives you peace and takes your mind off your worries. A study published in the JAMC showed how deep relaxation lowers blood pressure.[13] Scientists at various institutions have concluded that it boosts the immune system.[14] Emory University demonstrated results from a study that proved that it reduces inflammation. [15]

If you don't know how you can find time for relaxation with a hefty workload and a busy life, then consider the following. Besides the health benefits, it also increases your productivity and creativity. Once you relax, your senses heighten, and you become more aware of the bigger picture. You gain a fresh perspective on problems when you put them aside for a time. Suspending your thought gives your brain time to synthesize the information that it has taken in. You become emotionally balanced and less reactive to external stimuli. Relaxation is a powerful tool that is underutilized and overlooked in our hectic world but is also needed more now than ever.

Routines

There is a reason that Mark Zuckerberg, Steve Jobs, and many other highly successful people, including at least two of the most famous fashion designers, Michael Kohrs and Giorgio Armani, wear the same outfit every day. The principle behind this is the same reason that Nick Saban eats the same meal every day. Our mind has a finite amount of decisions that it is capable of processing at a high level every day. When it has reached the maximum amount that it can process, it is referred to as decision fatigue, as coined by social psychologist Roy F. Baumeister.[16] Logic shows that we are at our most mentally astute in the morning after the grogginess has cleared because we have made the least amount of decisions at this time. Successful people realize this and eliminate any decisions that they deem unnecessary to focus on what truly matters to them. Because of this, routines will dramatically increase our productivity throughout our days once they are in place because we will no longer be forced to make all these little decisions throughout our day. There is no single daily routine that is perfect for everyone. The important part is to outline a pattern and then stick with it so you can automate aspects of your life to reduce your decisions and focus on what truly matters to you. Make a routine that you will consistently keep. You can always add to or change it as you become more comfortable. In my interview with Roger Bartlett, he said, "I have a routine I do that is not so burdensome that I hate it and I don't want to do it anymore. You know it's just enough that I can keep it going." You can also design routines throughout other times of your day to get the maximum benefit out of this principle.

Goal Accountability

Goal accountability is an idea that I have wrestled with a great deal over time. I have experimented with sharing goals with people, as suggested by a study published in the Journal of Applied Psychology, *When goals are known: The effects of audience relative status on goal commitment and performance.*[17] I have also tried sharing my goals due to the study led by Peter Gollwitzer with the Department of Psychology at NYU.[18] Not happy with either of these conflicting studies, I then tried a mixture of the two. That is when I was able to receive the benefits of both methods.

Both telling people and not telling people have their benefits. When you tell someone the goal that you plan to see through, you may receive help from those who can assist you in an area. Those around you will also know to give you time and space to meet your needs. However, a con to telling people is that you will feel a sense of satisfaction from the excitement people show for your plan, and you haven't had to work for it. This is where keeping it to yourself would benefit you. When you're around people, and your goal is on your mind, and you can't talk about it, it builds a strong desire in you to get it done so that you can discuss it freely. You don't have the constant dopamine release of talking about what you're doing. Also, if you decide that the pursuit you begin is not worth your time and effort, you have no one to explain yourself to.

I have concluded that the best way to ensure finishing your goal is to combine these two philosophies. You will receive the benefits from each, without the adverse side effects. This is how it works:

1. Start working towards what you want to accomplish.
2. Determine whether or not it is worth continuing to pursue.
3. If it is worth your time, tell only those who can and will assist you in finishing.
4. Complete your goal, tell everyone, and reap the satisfaction of your hard work.

Daily Visualizing Practice

Visualize your end goal in full fruition. See in vivid detail what that looks like. Feel what it feels like to have everything completed. Practicing seeing what it looks like when everything is complete trains your subconscious to recognize opportunities that will arise to make your goal a reality sooner, causing you to gravitate towards them. What we think about most, we eventually become or achieve—because of this, vividly visualizing our goals each day is a simple yet powerful step. Visualizing has become a component of nearly all Olympian training regimens after the surprising statistics from studies on this subject. The Cleveland Clinic Foundation conducted a test where they asked participants to visualize flexing their biceps as hard as possible. After a few weeks, the results yielded an astounding 13.5% increase in strength.[19] The study conducted by the University of Chicago divided the subjects into 3 groups. They told the first group to practice shooting free throws for 1 hour every day for a month. They improved by 24%. They instructed the second group to visualize shooting free throws for a month without any physical practice. They improved their statistics by 23%. The third group was told not to visualize or physically practice free throws. They did not improve.[20]

Visualize in the morning and at night.

• Visualizing in the morning helps reinforce your focus to notice what will bring your goals closer throughout the day.

• Visualizing at night helps to connect proper synapses and synthesizes relevant information.

Short, Medium, and Long-Term Planning

5-Year Plan

Think back to the visualization technique that we did earlier in this book. What all did you see, feel, know, and have? 5 years is plenty of time to accomplish many of your desired goals. I encourage you to get out a pen and paper for this exercise to create a mind map. For this mind map, the central idea is "5-year Goals." Stemming from that, you can put a word from the following prompts I give you and any others you may think of in this process. Think about the different facets of your life. What are your relationships like? What career do you have, and how well are you performing? What does your physical health look like? What do you do on a day to day basis? Do you have a daily routine? What skills do you have that you enjoy doing? How are you spiritually? What impact do you have on the society around you? Who are you helping in some way, be it mentoring or volunteering or any other form? These are just a few ideas to get you started seriously visualizing your ideal future.

After you have written everything that has come to mind, put a star next to the top 3 that are most important to you. Put a triangle next to any that logically seem to be a necessary next goal in the future. These may overlap with the ones that are stars, which would work out great for you. Here is an example.

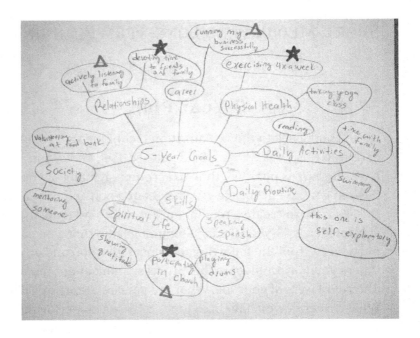

Next, divide another piece of paper into three sections with two lines going all the way down. Write the 3 goals that you starred. Below those, put any of your other goals that would logically go before those to save you time and make your starred goal more attainable.

10-Year Plan

I have seen many people start with their 10-year plan and work backward. That is fine, but I have found that it is more effective to work the other way. Starting out planning your goals at a time in the much nearer future will allow you to have a more accurate idea of what you will actually be able to accomplish. When we don't reach the goals we set out for, it can discourage us. A lot can happen in 10 years that we cannot even come close to predicting. Already having your 5-year plan in place gives you a starting trajectory for where your 10-year plan can take you. But let's take a different approach to how we see our lives in 10 years. Our perspective is everything. It's how our world is shaped in our minds. Disappointment in goal setting is merely the difference between what we expect and how reality manifests itself. For our 10-year perspective, pick massive goals. Make them larger than what you expect to accomplish. Have the ideas in your head and a clear vision of what this is but remember that it is far bigger than what you realistically expect. These giant goals will work like a magnet to pull you towards your realistic goals without disappointment if you don't reach them. The bigger you think, the more creatively your mind will have to work to generate solutions to get you to your goals. This is how the giant goals work as a magnet. You think bigger than the issues at hand, and it pulls you through the struggles and obstacles you will inevitably face along the way.

"The greater danger for most of us lies not in setting our aim too high and falling short; but in setting our aim too low and achieving our mark. "[21]

- Michelangelo

7 FACETS OF LIFE THAT PLAY INTO ALL GOALS

What I'm about to write may not be what you were hoping or expected to hear. However, my goal is to help as many people as I can. It's not writing what they want to hear so I can go viral. Here it goes. The hustle culture that promotes working 25-hour days 8 days a week is absolutely wrong when it promises that it will all be worth it.

I heard Nathan Caldwell, author of *Empowering Kindness: Why Unlocking Power in Others Will Be Your Greatest Success*, capture this point perfectly when he told the following story.

Caldwell recently had the opportunity to interview a world-renowned public speaker with a massive following. Caldwell asked this highly influential public figure for some advice on how to land more speaking events himself. The man explained that when he was first starting, he quit his job, took out a mortgage on his house, and had just enough money to survive for 18 months. He knew he had to work hard to become successful before the 18 months were over. He told Caldwell that he achieved success within that time period by working non-stop. However, he also went through a divorce and lost touch with his kids.

What good did wasting all that time and severing the ties with his family do? What good is having all the money and fame in the world when we give up two much more valuable parts of our lives (time and relationships)? Sustainable happiness cannot be found unless there is a balance in our lives. There's nothing wrong with making millions of dollars or being highly influential. The problem arises when we sacrifice what truly matters in the process. No matter how ambitious the goals are we accomplish, they will not bring us happiness unless they align with our true values.

Relationship of Goals and Habits

For any success, there isn't just one tactic that will get you there. Successes are intricate processes made up of many essential components. Two of the most essential aspects are goals and habits. Goals and habits are meant to live in harmony. The goal is the finished structure of what we want to accomplish, and the habits are the bricks we lay to finish it. One without the other leads to a site that will remain under construction for years until it finally falls apart.

Fortunately, like any architect, we can be trained in the proper procedures to build the most magnificent structure that our minds can dream up. Success is a learnable process.

We all possess habits; some help to serve us well while others hold us back. We are the culmination of our habits. What we do every day is an immediate impression of the state and nature of our lives. So, it's a given that individuals who need to improve their lives and accomplish their objectives need to make and implement a well-crafted set of habits. As one of my truest friends, Noah Hightower, once said, "Successful people make a habit of doing things that others are unwilling to do."

No matter what our goal is, all the facets of our life will be affected by it to one degree or another. The habits that build up each pillar are interconnected, creating a compounding effect on the success of the goal we are currently achieving, and any goals to come. For example, our physical health has a dramatic impact on our mental health, which in turn affects how we treat others around us, how well we perform at work, our ability to serve our social roles such as mentoring, volunteering, and so on. Our financial status can affect what types of foods we can afford. The more money we have, the more freedom of time we have to spend with our family and friends if we so choose to. There are many other connections that I'm sure you can make yourself. From this, you can also see how the habits have a compounding effect on goals we will be working towards.

Every goal is different and will, therefore, require different habits. Listed below are habits that are so fundamental that they will likely affect whatever goal it is. They will all either save you time, give you more energy, reduce your stress, give you a vast amount of freedom, or provide more than one of these benefits.

Live an Intentional Life

Because we have a limited amount of time, money, and energy, how we allocate them is incredibly important. If we make our decisions based on what is popular around us and what we believe will make us appear successful to others, then no matter what we achieve, we will always feel a sense of inadequacy. Success looks different to all people, and therefore we will never be able to please everyone. In my interview with Roger Bartlett, the original guitarist in Jimmy Buffet's Coral Reefer Band, he addressed this issue in the best way possible with his following analogy.

"Success is a relative thing. If a hedge fund manager were to come to me and say, 'you're not a successful guy, you don't have any money like I have.' I would say to him, 'No, you're not a successful guy because you don't have any Gold Records and you can't play any instruments. It's all what you value. People see things through the prism of their own experience, so whatever you value, you tend to impose on other people to judge their success, but I think that is a false equivalency."

What brings you fulfillment in all the facets of your life? Are you happy with the balance that you currently have? If not, then change it based on your core values. We find fulfillment when our values inside our minds are in alignment with the reality on the outside. We will need to revisit this alignment from time to time as we mature because our core values will, in turn, mature with us.

What success is can look different to anyone, but these habits are necessary to lay a solid foundation on which we can build our goals.

CAREER

Out of all of the activities in our lives, our careers will typically be where we allocate the most time. Making the most of this time will affect our moods when we are outside of work and our financial wellbeing.

Boss Mentality

Make all of your decisions at work with the mindset that you own the company. Not only will this make you better at your job, but it will also make you stand out above employees who only think about the task at hand and don't have a good grasp on the bigger picture. It gives you a better appreciation for where you work and why you are doing what you do. Knowing this helps the menial tasks we can get stuck with more bearable. This mindset will help you see what is truly important and put those tasks first.

This has always been the mindset I have striven for in all of my various jobs, and it has worked well for me. But I gained a deeper appreciation for it after reading *It's Your Ship* by Captain Abrashoff. He tells how he took command of the worst ship in the navy and transformed it into arguably the best. He attributes much of the success to his mindset. He explains, "I put myself in the shoes of my boss" ... "I also made sure to act in the least threatening manner possible. None of my actions could possibly bankrupt the company or hurt anyone's career. I took prudent, calculated risks, the kind I thought my boss would want me to take."[1]

Later he gives an example of how having this boss mentality pays off. "The whole exercise in thinking like my bosses paid off when Secretary Perry had me fly to the Middle East for a series of crisis meetings on 6 hours' notice, and I had to arrange the whole trip." He details how he had to delegate tasks for arranging the trip and says, "I had to laugh. These guys were all the civilian equivalents of four-star generals, and I was a lowly Navy commander making half their salaries, but they were standing there expecting me to take the lead. So, I started giving them assignments... and because I had learned to think like my bosses, I knew what those things were."[2]

Why is this important?

- Stand out above the competition
- Provides work satisfaction
- Increases productivity

Networking

Networking, in this sense, is a term first used in 1985 to describe the act of building a business network by connecting people. You have likely come across this idea, but why is it vital for us, and how do we do it? In the simplest form, networking is building social capital. These are still human relationships, and we should, therefore, treat them as such. Relationships need to be beneficial to both parties involved. Avoid social-leeches, those who only seek to benefit themselves, and most especially avoid being one. First, seek to help others, and then they will be more inclined to help you. Leave everyone better off than when you met them. Networking doesn't just happen at classified mixers. It can happen anywhere you meet someone. There are opportunities all around us if we keep our eyes open. You can also find specialty events in areas that interest you. These events can be great places to meet people in your field. You may receive valuable career advice from someone advanced in your field. You may be more specialized in an area than they are and could greatly benefit them now or when a job opens up in the future. These relationships build leverage for everyone. You can benefit from each other's strengths and accelerate your growth far quicker than either of you could alone. If you are going into a mixer, here are the steps to take to build quality connections.

Steps

1. Be approachable. If your body language is closed off and you're standing in a corner, don't expect to make connections.

2. Don't avoid people on the basis that they aren't high enough up the ladder. You never know what you can learn from someone or who they may be connected to. You also don't know how far their career may skyrocket one day.

3. Have it in your head to learn about the other person and be genuinely interested in them. Everyone has a story to tell.

4. Ask questions. Investigate and find out their story. Bring out the best in everybody you meet.

5. When it comes to value, offer value first. When you're listening to them, listen for a problem that you may be able to help them with. If you don't have the answer yourself, refer them to a resource or a person who can help them. If they are like most people, they'll offer value in return either at that time or later. If not, you still had the opportunity to help someone.

6. Create a lasting memory with the help you give them and your genuine care for their wellbeing.

Why?

- Can get you out of your comfort zone and expand your horizons

- Accelerates growth

- Job opportunities

- Social proof with recommendations from the people you meet

- A chance to help someone

- Career advice from people with experience

Learning and Adapting

Whatever job you find yourself in, being in the habit of adapting will allow you to stand out above the rest. This is true whether you work for someone or you are independent. Learning quickly will allow you to save an incredible amount of time on learning new skills that will enhance your ability to do your current job or add skills that will open new careers to you. As quickly as the world is advancing, without the ability to quickly learn and adapt, you are in great danger of falling behind and being replaced either by someone who has these habits or a machine. Adapting also allows you to become more efficient in the skills you currently do have.

The first step is to be aware of this need and to be on the lookout for how you can adapt. Once you have decided on a necessary skill, determine the extent to which you need to learn it in order to serve your situation. Once you know to what degree learning this skill will benefit you, break it down into smaller sub-skills. Prioritize these subskills based on your needs. Pick out time for when you are going to practice them. Deliberately practice each of these subskills until you are aware of what you are doing right and what you are doing wrong. Find more than one source to learn the skill from because everyone has a different teaching style, and one will be easier for us to relate to than the others. Find experts on this subject and analyze their techniques.

Why?

- Saves a significant amount of time

- Job security

- New job opportunities

- Improve your own business quickly

FINANCE

Our financial status has a large impact on our opportunities. The more financial resources we have, the more we are free to utilize our time how we would like. This could mean spending more time developing our relationships, concentrating more on our health, or however we would like to use our freedom. It also allows more access to learning materials, healthier foods, and other luxuries of life.

Emergency Fund

If we don't have an emergency fund in place or enough available cash when something requiring it happens, we could have a problem. Emergencies could be a necessary medical operation, a job loss, home, or car repair, to name a few. Whatever the situation we find ourselves in, we can be prepared for it. Being prepared goes back to the proactive versus reactive mindset. We need to be ready so that we will be able to take care of ourselves and others when life inevitably happens. Dave Ramsey says that when we are financially prepared, "an emergency becomes an inconvenience."[3] An emergency fund is something that may take a few months of savings to build but will be worth the peace of mind and freedom it provides. The amount will vary for everyone, but a good rule of thumb that many financial advisors recommend is 3 months' worth of living expenses. It is also recommended to have a separate account for this money, so you are not tempted to use it for less than an emergency.

Why?

- Peace of mind

- Help others

- Freedom

Save Your Money Like the Bank, Not Just In It

Many of us put our money into a savings account, but what happens to it once it's there? Do the bankers just put our money under their mattresses and guard it for us for free? Of course not. Most people don't know much about what happens with their money once it is in their bank's possession. The main thing people do know about how the bank uses it is to give out loans and charge a high interest rate. A lesser-known use is that the banks are investing our money and getting an average of 11.39% ROE[4] while giving us 1% on our investment. So how do we get a higher return on our money? Instead of putting the money that we are saving into a savings account, we should put it where the bank does.

Investing may be a foreign concept to you if we have always put our money in savings. There are many ways to invest your money. Spend a couple of hours seeing what would fit your situation the best. That small amount of time will pay you back many times over. There are so many intricacies to consider while investing, and the stock market is an ever-changing place. Not everyone wants to spend much time working in this area. If that is you, consider getting a financial advisor. They will receive a percentage of your return on investment but will save you the time spent investigating and learning the trade. Besides saving you time and uncovering better investments, having a financial advisor will also keep you from making emotional decisions. They study the market and make their decisions based on years of experience and logic, not emotional whims. A financial advisor is not a lifetime commitment. You can start there, learn from the experience, and take that with you to invest on your own if you so choose.

Why?

- Continually grow your wealth

- Learn a new skill

- Build money for retirement

- Reach financial goals

- Be able to support others

Multiple Sources of Income

In "Rich Habits,"[5] Tom Corley describes the lessons he learned from studying the habits of millionaires for 5 years. Here are the statistics he found on multiple sources of income:

- 65% of self-made millionaires had three streams of income.

- 45% of self-made millionaires had four streams of income.

- 29% of self-made millionaires had five or more streams of income.

Having money coming in is an essential wealth-building habit and is necessary for financial security in these volatile times. With the high risk of companies going bankrupt, machines replacing jobs, or more unforeseen events such as the virus epidemic in 2020 leading to loss of work, we cannot be entirely reliant on money coming from our primary job. These do not have to be multiple full-time jobs. It would be hard to live a balanced life if that were the case. These can be as simple as setting up the ability to make money in a different way than you currently are. You can set up sources of passive income cultivated to correspond with your current skills or ones you learn for this purpose.

Why?

- Financial freedom

- Ability to support others

- Job security

HEALTH

We only get one body. It is the hardware, and our mind is the software. We take such great care of our phones, buying cases and screen covers for them even though we can always buy another one. We continue to update them to the latest software available. Since we only get one body, it seems that we should do what we can to continually care for it and protect it the best to the best of our abilities. The following fundamental habits will lay a solid foundation for just that. Consult your doctor before making these wonderful lifestyle changes.

Sleep, QUALITY Sleep

Quality sleep is a habit that could go under virtually any of the categories because of its impact on every aspect of our lives. There's a good reason that we are recommended to spend 1/3 of every day doing it, and it seems like, with that much practice, we would all be a lot better at it.

Reduce technology use for 1 hour prior to falling asleep. The blue light that protrudes from screens is highly detrimental to your sleep quality.

Make sure you are getting enough magnesium during the day. Magnesium works synergistically with melatonin to help regulate your sleep-wake cycle. It also helps regulate your neurotransmitters allowing your nervous system to calm when it's time to sleep.

Get enough sunlight in the morning. Exposure to the sun increases melatonin levels.

Wake up at the same time every day, even on weekends... Your body gets used to the routine, which is evident through the circadian rhythm. The circadian rhythm tells your body when to release the melatonin you worked so hard for in the previous step, and it will do so on 24-hour intervals.

Why

- Improved memory along with many other mental functions

- Lower blood pressure

- Better mood

- Maintain a healthy weight

- Allows the body to repair itself

Basics nutritional needs

In our ever increasingly busy lives, it is hard to always get the nutrients we need. But the busier we get, the more crucial it is for our bodies and minds to be at their peak capacity. I have compiled a list of the major nutrients our bodies need. Natural sources are always the best to get these from, but not always easily accessible. If you cannot get them from natural sources, then vitamins and powders are much better than nothing. If you have not been getting sufficient nutrients, then expect to feel significant effects from it in about a month.

WebMD[6] is an excellent source to determine the amount of nutrients needed daily for each individual's needs.

Vitamins:

A, B1, B2, B3, B5, B6, B7, B9, B12, C, D, E, and K

Minerals:

Major Minerals: calcium, phosphorus, potassium, sodium, and magnesium

Trace Minerals: sulfur, iron, chlorine, cobalt, copper, zinc, manganese, molybdenum, iodine, and selenium.

Proteins:

This is a slightly more complex topic. The amino acids that build the proteins our bodies need can be found in different types of food, but if you don't have time for that, then protein powder is a great supplement. Protein powders are not just made for heavy lifters. Our bodies are all made up of the same basic components, so protein powders will benefit everybody. If you are going to go this route, then these are the essential 9 amino acids to look for that will give your body the protein it needs: histidine, isoleucine, leucine, lysine, methionine, phenylalanine, threonine, tryptophan, and valine.

Fats Sources:

Avocados, Olive oil, Nuts, Eggs, Fatty Fish, coconut oil, and Krill oil pills

Why?

- Improved cognitive abilities

- Improved energy levels

- Better mood

- Higher sleep quality

- Boosts productivity

Daily Exercise

"If there were a drug that could do for human health everything that exercise can, it would likely be the most valuable pharmaceutical ever developed," -Dr. Mark Tarnapolsky.[7] Why is this? Exercise is one of the most intertangled habits with the others in its overall compounding effect. Exercise enhances our learning capacity by producing Brain-Derived Neurotrophic Factor (BDNF).[8]

For the brain to learn anything, it has to change how it is structured and grow. BDNF stimulates the same brain growth that is needed for learning. Harvard Psychiatrist John Ratey M.D. called BDNF "a crucial biological link between thought, emotions, and movement."[9] Exercising doesn't mean you have to run a marathon or do heavy weightlifting. A study in the Journal of Sports Science and Medicine explained 20-40 minutes of aerobic exercise a day increased BDNF in the blood by 32%.[10] 20-40 minutes is also enough time to oxygenate your blood and to boost your endorphins. Exercise increases our motivation by triggering the release of dopamine. It also combats depression by elevating our levels of norepinephrine and serotonin. The type and difficulty of the exercise are dependent on the needs and abilities of the individual, but everybody can do this.

Why?

- Improves insulin sensitivity

- Dopamine, oxytocin, and serotonin are released

- Gives mental clarity

- Gives energy

- Helps you sleep

- More emotionally sound

- Reduces stress

- Increases focus

Watch what you eat

Everyone knows sugar is bad for you, but not all understand the magnitude of this truth. Sugar is poison. Eating sugar is linked to the development of diabetes. It is also what cancer cells feed on to reproduce in our bodies. It leads to weight gain, heart disease, high blood pressure, and diminishes the acetylcholine level in our brains. Acetylcholine is the neurotransmitter responsible for motivation, attention, learning, and memory. After these diminish, the pancreas produces high insulin levels, which results in the storage of fat cells and eventually degenerating the pancreas. This destruction of the pancreas is what leads to type 2 diabetes. The high consumption of sugar greatly hinders our minds. Eating sugar triggers a quick release of dopamine by our brains. However, when a high amount of sugar is stored, this leads to a decrease in dopamine levels and low levels of energy.

Why?

- High and sustainable energy levels

- Healthy weight loss

- Increased brain function

- Absorption of vitamins and minerals

Drink Water

Many people talk about how we need to drink water. They explain that our body is made up of approximately 60% water. They say we need to take how many pounds we weigh, divide that by two, and that is how many ounces of water we need to drink daily. That is all true, but what are the benefits of drinking enough water? That is what we will discuss here. Drinking water clears the body of toxins and reduces swelling. Drinking water on an empty stomach stimulates the growth of red blood cells, leading to higher oxygenation in our blood, which increases our energy. Water is essential for the health of our immune system. Drinking warm water improves circulation and detoxification.[11] It has also been shown to increase weight loss more so than cold water.[12] A study done by the European Journal of Pharmaceutical and Medical Research concluded that drinking ice water constricts the blood vessels and leads to improper digestion.[13] Anyone who understands the basic science behind molecules expanding or contracting due to the temperature can see the logic behind this. However, many people still drink ice cold water. The study also reveals that "adding ice to processed cold water will strip it of natural-containing minerals, as these minerals are essential to keeping the digestive tract healthy." It is still much better than alternative drinks, but even the way we drink it can be improved. Not enough water can lead to us craving sugar, which we know how detrimental giving into this craving is for our health.

Why?

- Higher Metabolic rate

- Proper digestion

- Increased energy

- Aids in weight loss

- Improved immune system

- Lower blood pressure

- Lubricates joints

- Boosts skin health

- Flushes toxins

MENTALITY

There are so many ads going around promoting claims that their products will improve the functionality of the user's brains. For a small fee each month, they promise to increase your memory, concentration, etc. Let's discuss some fundamental habits scientifically proven that you can implement right now to improve your overall mentality for free.

Take a walk

Out of all the research I did on the most powerful and fundamental habits in all of the 7 facets of life, the results from the studies I found on this simple habit surprised me the most. It is humorous to me the length to which people will go to try and get an edge on their mental abilities while overlooking the simplest things, myself included. It may be that people are genuinely unaware of the overwhelming benefits that come from these simple actions. Nonetheless, nootropics (smart drugs) have become all the rage without much evidence to back up many of the claimed benefits or to prove that there are no long-term side effects. With that in mind, in a study done by Stanford University, the benefits of walking were tested, and concluded that it increases creativity in the brain by 60%.[14] So, the bottom line is, your dog just really cares about your mental health. This increase in creativity alone would be enough motivation to get people to walk, but that isn't the only benefit.

Why?

- Increased circulation

- Improved sleep

- Joint support

- Healthy weight

- Heart disease prevention

- Muscle strengthening

- Lowered risk of Alzheimer's

- Increased strength

- Lowered blood sugar

This is starting to sound like a list at the end of a medicine commercial, except these are all positive side effects!

Deep Work

Deep work, simply stated, is an extended period of time in which you eliminate any potential distractions and concentrate on a single task. It may sound daunting at first, but it's something you can gradually build up to. In Cal Newport's bestselling book, "Deep Work: Rules for Focused Success in a Distracted World," he writes that when first starting, a person can typically only perform 1 hour of successful deep work a day. He also explains that the upper threshold for those who have been practicing it for years is 4 hours. [15] That 4 hours of deep work is much more productive than a typical worker's 12 hours of a normal day.

Plan the night before what you are going to work on and set out any necessary materials. Block out a time in the day for it. For our purposes, this should be the time you have allotted for working on your goal. Eliminate anything that could distract you. Turn off your phone. If you're working on the computer, don't get on Facebook or your email. Inform anyone that may try to talk to you about what you are doing. Studies have shown that after your mind switches focus even momentarily, it takes roughly 20 minutes for the subconscious to stop allocating some of its resources and energy to whatever it was on, and return your attention entirely back to the main task. Using this method instead of Pomodoro (set intervals of working and relaxing) eliminates the need to motivate yourself to start so many times in the same day. You have fewer chances to get sucked in by the distractions because you don't allow yourself all of the breaks.

Why?

- Gives you time in the day after you work to use for other purposes

- Eliminates the need to start again and again

- Gives your brain time to get deep into your work

- Increases creativity

Heart Rate Variability Training

Heart rate variability (HRV) is precisely what it sounds like. A higher variability means having a shorter and a longer pause between the beats. Heart rate speeds up when you inhale and slows down when you exhale. A smooth variation is a good thing. It shows that your heart is getting signals from both the sympathetic (fight or flight) and the parasympathetic system (rest and relax). People with higher heart rate variability are better at dealing with stress, staying focused, and delaying instant gratification.[16] Because of this, Kelly McGonigal Ph.D. refers to HRV as the body's reserve of will power in *The Willpower Instinct*. When a stressful situation occurs, our bodies go into fight-or-flight mode. In this mode, our energy is directed to our bodies to help us fight or run. This takes the energy away from the brain. Having control over our HRV allows us to go into something psychologist Suzanne Segerstrom calls the pause-and-plan response. This response is initiated by the prefrontal cortex when it identifies that another part of the brain wants to do something now that will not help in the long run. Our ability to control our HRV does not mean that when we require a quick response to face a threat that we will react slowly. In training our HRV, we retain our reaction time while simultaneously having the ability to remain rational. The stress that we experience in our lives is typically not life-threatening. Pioneer in HRV research, Dr. Richard Gevirtz explained, "If you're mildly stressed all day long, no major emergencies... that is more harmful than big major emergency stressors that you get over quickly."[17]

This is how to train our heart rate variability:

1. Stay hydrated.
2. Eat the necessary nutrients.
3. Get quality sleep.
4. Use modalities of recovery such as massages, saunas, ice-baths, etc.
5. Practice breathwork. The optimal breathing rate for individuals differs from person to person. You can find yours by using a biofeedback device. If you do not have access to one, you can use the average breathing rate, which is exhaling for 5 seconds and then inhaling for 5 seconds. Doing this for 10 minutes, puts your body into a state of coherence. Coherence is when your heart rate, blood pressure, and respiration are all synchronized.

Why?

- Stronger will power

- Pain management

- Reduces symptoms of asthma

- Helps alleviate depression

- Increases self-control

- Decreases sleep latency

- Develops emotional control

- Lowers blood pressure

MINDFULNESS

For all facets of our lives, building a solid foundation is necessary. But no other pillar has as great of an impact on our overall happiness as mindfulness. When we are grateful for what we have been given, learn to engage in the present moment, and gain control over our happiness, we will be able to put our lives into perspective. Happiness and peace become a choice. We understand how to find joy in the present, and that puts any negatives into perspective. We respond wisely to our emotions and external stimuli instead of reacting blindly. We learn to live in alignment with our moral values, and we find peace.

Mind Dump

Have you ever experienced something popping in your head that you know you need to get done, but you are trying to focus on something else at the time? Or have you ever been exhausted at the end of the day, lie in bed, and thoughts keep coming to your mind? If so, then it is time for a mind dump. Your mind is for creating ideas, not holding them in. Write down everything you need to do, are constantly thinking about, are stressed about, thoughts, tasks, fears, questions, and worries. The point is to get these things out of your mind and onto the paper. Export the information in your brain to another place of storage. Make sure you use an actual piece of paper instead of typing it because physically transcribing your thoughts has a substantial impact on getting it out of your brain and on to something else.

Dumping all of your thoughts out is not the time to organize or prioritize. No thoughts you write are too big or too small. They can be very specific or vague. If in the time you have allotted for doing a mind dump, you experience writer's block, try walking around your home or your office to try and trigger ideas about what needs to be done.

After it's all stored on the paper, take a deep breath in and exhale slowly. Now it is time to organize what you have written. Put whatever you wrote that you need to do on your to-do list or schedule for the next week. If it's a goal, write it on your goals list. If it's a memory, write it in your journal. You can organize whatever else you wrote into specialized lists. After seeing these long lists, it may seem overwhelming. However, it should be encouraging because your mind is no longer holding onto them while trying to remember and process everything else.

Why?

- Trade mental clutter for mental clarity

- Mindfulness

- Focus

- Aids productivity and reduces stress

Meditate

Meditation comes in many forms, but the key is to practice focusing on one thing at a time. Train your mind not to wander when you are not allowing it to. The following is my preferred method to start the morning, but if you have a different approach, then that can work just as well.

1. Compassion: Focus on having compassion for all of those around you and be very visual about this. Imagine yourself having compassion for the people in the house that you live in. Then imagine walking around your neighborhood and having compassion for everyone there. Imagine having compassion for everyone in the city you live in and then bringing it to the state, country, and lastly, the world.

2. Thankfulness: Imagine in detail all the things that you are thankful for. This one is pretty straightforward.

3. Forgiveness: Forgiving someone to their face is the first step, but it will still hurt us if we continue to hold onto it. Think about someone you have some underlying hard feelings towards, visualize yourself forgiving them, and then think of something that you may have done wrong to them and apologize. If you can honestly think of no one, move on to the next step.

4. Ideal Day: Visualize your whole day starting where you are right now to the end of it. Imagine exactly how you would like everything to go. Visualize even your physiology as you're going throughout the day and imagine the most productive way you can go about everything until the moment that you hit your head on your pillow.

5. Your ideal future. As vividly as possible, imagine how you would like to be living in 10 years from now. Imagine your ideal life as detailed as possible, including your job,

family life, skills you possess, and whatever else is important to you.

6. Self-efficacy practice. Think of three things about yourself that you are proud of.

7. Pray. Here we put life into perspective, realize how small we are, and express our gratefulness.

Why?

• Meditation benefits

• Lowers the level of stress hormones

• Boosts immune system

• Mitigates depression, anxiety, ADHD, and age-related cognitive decline

• Meta skill that improves everything else

Journaling

After an in-depth look into what common factors are shared by the most successful people of today and the past, the act of journaling proved to be one of the most consistent and tangible links. Most successful people today didn't write their journals because they knew they would one day be successful; rather, they turned out to be successful in part because they journaled. Studies show that we have over 6,200 thoughts in a single day.[18] With all of these thoughts, it's no wonder that we can feel overwhelmed and not know which of these ideas to pursue or the fact that our brains are constantly bouncing from one idea to another. Our mind is like an attic into which we keep throwing our junk, and we eventually don't know what all is up there. This is where journaling becomes so helpful. It forces us to slow down and only think about one idea at a time. When we begin writing, we are slowly taking our stuff out of the attic and examining it to find out what matters. The ideas that we write down and decide are not worth our time we can now throw away. We can examine our fears and stresses by writing them down and rationally selecting solutions. What you write is ultimately up to you, but some helpful things to consider are your goals, desires, fears, things you need to do, what you are thankful for, and reflections from the day. It helps you to figure out where you are expending your mental energy and what your values are. Putting your thoughts on paper allows you to articulate them in an understandable way and will improve your communication skills. Journaling physically changes the structure of our brains. Specifically, researchers found that the brains of people who journaled about what they were grateful for were changed by the end of the 3-week test. The MRI scans showed that in the ventromedial prefrontal cortex (the same region of the brain that is associated with altruism) showed more efficiency in the oxygen metabolism of the cells, a critical process for cognitive function.

Why?

- Memory and learning are improved

- Reduces cortisol, leading to lower levels of stress, anxiety, and depression

- Declutters your mind

- Improves decision-making ability

- Improves communication skills

Being Present

I have heard many people claim to be multitaskers despite the large amount of conclusive evidence denying that as a possibility. However, these same people are indeed much better at switching exceptionally quickly from one thing to another. Over time, this constant rapid switching without stopping to be in the present causes our minds to undergo fatigue. This fatigue is especially apparent when it comes to the things that we are worried about. Being present is a term that people have started throwing around in recent years, but what does it really mean? Being present is being completely aware of the moment that you are in, including how you feel. You are not distracted by worries of the future or the past. This awareness gives you the power to be in control of your thoughts and emotions. We don't have control over the past. We can't change it. And despite how much we may think we can control the future, there will always be external forces we cannot predict. The danger of not being present is letting our lives pass us by. We only get each moment once. The more distracted we are, the more likely we are to react to the things happening around us without thinking logically. How do you practice being present? For now, take deep breaths, notice how your body feels, and focus on what you are doing. Doing this and experiencing what it feels like will cause it to become easier and more natural over time. If you have thoughts other than what you are doing right now, imagine your thoughts tied to helium balloons and floating away.

Why?

- Improved listening skills

- Better memory

- More meticulous work

- Control of our emotions

- Much easier to get into flow

- Increased efficiency

Relationships

A study published in the PLOS Medicine Journal concluded that lack of quality relationships is killing us faster than lack of exercise or obesity![19] As John Donne stated, "No man is an island, entire of itself; every man is a piece of the Continent, a part of the main." All aspects of our life are much more enjoyable and complete when it is filled with dependable people.

Listen

Listen to hear; don't listen to answer. If you're listening to respond and not listening to hear, then you won't know why the speaker is telling you something, and you might miss a critical point. Not listening attentively is the number one reason for poor communication. Listening is a choice, and it takes practice to do well. However, it is not a complicated mystery, as we sometimes imagine it to be. It involves both verbal and nonverbal communication. Psychology follows physiology and vice versa, so both aspects are essential. If we have open body language and maintain eye contact, this signals to our brain to listen. Go into conversations with the mindset of an investigator. Find out what is important to whom you are talking and let them tell their story. Ask thoughtful questions that are related to what they are talking about. Pay attention to their nonverbal communication, too. Their mood and intentions are just as crucial to the message they are presenting as the words they are saying.

Why?

- Shows respect

- Everyone has something to teach us

- People need to be heard

- Better communication

Help

Not only is helping others the right thing to do, but you have strengths that others do not, and they will be more willing to help you down the road if they see you're genuinely interested in helping them. Being genuine is the crucial part, and not because you want something in return. This journey we are on is much easier when we don't walk it alone. Everyone has something that they need. When we see a need, we should we willing to do what we can for them. It may be easier to give a man a fish than to teach him to fish, but as the Chinese proverb tells us, teaching him to fish will feed him for a lifetime. I believe this is highlighting the effect of collaboration. If we collaborate with someone to meet their need instead of merely solving it for them, they will be involved in the process and be more able to replicate it in the future. This new skill they have, combined with the compassion they receive from you, will make them willing to help others around them. When they help someone else, this will have a ripple effect that will continue on and improve many lives from this single act.

Why?

- It's the right thing to do

- It improves our mood

- We will need help later on

Patient Perspective

When we pause to put things into perspective, we realize that most momentary annoyances we experience are not as big of a deal as we first imagined. Furthermore, there are likely many times we have needed others to be patient with us. The underlying reason our friend does or says something is not always apparent. If it is something that bothers us, we need to be patient to find out their reasoning and be willing to take the time to investigate what is going on behind the scenes. Don't assume you know the answer: ask. They are not always going to see things the same way we do. We all look at situations from our own perspectives and pasts that shape how we think. We can use these differences to better each other through our strengths if we are willing to take a step back from the moment and exhibit a patient perspective.

Society

Whether it's a charity you donate to, deciding to recycle your bottle or any other action that affects society, you are contributing to the quality of the world we live in. Some people are so self-absorbed they don't consider how their actions affect others, but consciously or not, they are still impacting society. As Bill Maher put it, "Not doing anything is doing something and choosing to look away is a passive but no less mortal sin."[20] When we are good stewards of what we have and consider how our actions will impact others now and in the future, we will then live in harmony. For our purposes, we are only discussing habits that will help us establish our pillars in a way that will help us reach our goals, and that is why I focused on the following.

The Law of 33%

You may know who Tai Lopez is. No matter your opinion of him and his ads, he does provide useful nuggets of wisdom. One of those times was with his 33% Rule.[21] The idea behind this rule is to divide our social time into three sections. One of these sections is with people who will mentor us in areas of life that we respect them for and desire to have developed in our own lives. The second section is with our peers- typically, our closest friends. These are people who are healthy to have in our lives, and we enjoy spending time with them. The last section involves people we can help mentor, including those that are younger than us, or not as developed in areas as we are. None of us got where we are in our lives today by ourselves. Undoubtedly, there were people that helped us along the way. All of us have something we can offer to others. It is when we realize this that we can begin to grow dramatically and help others along their journeys.

Section 1: Finding Mentors

My motivation in seeking the wisdom of successful people in various fields for this book sprang from my believe that the value of a good mentor is priceless. A mentor is typically someone who has taken the path you wish to take in a particular area of life and is years past where you currently are. They have been in your shoes and overcome many of the obstacles that you will inevitably face.

Looking at some of the most successful people, we can see that being mentored is a proven practice. Warren Buffet was mentored by Benjamin Graham. Bill Gates was mentored by Paul Allen. Alexander the Great was mentored by Aristotle. Mark Zuckerberg was mentored by Steve Jobs. These are just a fraction of the examples I found while looking into this.

There is value in having multiple mentors. No one person is an expert in every field. You probably wouldn't ask Warren Buffet how to work out or Arnold Schwarzenegger what stocks to invest in.

Speaking of these two leaders in their fields, imagine having them sitting down in your living room talking to you and telling you their paths to success. How beneficial would that be to you? Imagine Bill Gates, Steve Jobs, Thomas Edison, or Sam Walton having coffee with you for a couple of hours. How much wisdom could you glean from them, and how much time would that save you on your own journey? The great news is that in a sense, you can! Reading books is one of the most valuable ways you can spend your time, and it is so often overlooked. Sadly, many people have told me they don't have time to read. The very people who say this are the very ones who would benefit most from reading books. The time spent with the words transcribed by the most brilliant minds that have lived before us will return you that investment many times over.

You can live your life and try to do everything on your own and learn from your own mistakes. Or you could invest a small amount of time in reading, avoid many of the obstacles and blunders you would make on your own, and have much more time to work efficiently. Warren Buffet once said, "It's good to learn from your mistakes. It's better to learn from other people's mistakes."[22] Sam Walton was still humble enough to learn from others when he was already a billionaire in his 60s! One night, Sam Walton's friends got a call from the police station in South America. Walton had been arrested for crawling on his hands and knees in multiple retail stores with a measuring tape. He later explained to his friends that he was trying to learn from the Brazilian retail stores to see if he could improve the layout of his already incredibly successful empire of Walmart stores.[23]

Section 2: Friends

You become the average of your 5 closest friends. They shape what you do, how you talk, what you think about, and your attitude. Our minds take in all of the things we hear and see regularly. We don't always think about our friends in this way, but people are creatures of conformity. Even how we feel is heavily influenced by our friends. The effect that toxic people have on us is much more apparent. It's a draining feeling constantly being around negativity.

We experience the opposite when we are with those who are always smiling and in a good mood. We feel energized and see the world in a brighter light. The extreme ends of the spectrum make this truth more obvious, but just because the effects of the middle of the scale are harder to realize, does not make them any less relevant. Depending on what spectrum we measure, whether it is positivity/negativity, problem-solving/problem-blaming, self-control/indulgence, constant exposure to any of these or others will dramatically impact our own scales. We will become desensitized to it, whether good or bad, and it will become our norm. Wherever the average of our friends is on these scales is where we will drift to as well. It is not selfish to pick our friends wisely and withdraw ourselves from negative influences. It is the opposite, in fact, because we will be exposing our family to these behaviors, whether directly through the people we bring around them or the newly added behaviors in your own repertoire. Just like in nature, a relationship that is only beneficial in one direction and harmful in the other is a parasitic relationship. Needless to say, this is not what you are looking for. Symbiotic relationships are the type we need to keep and cultivate in our lives. These relationships are mutually beneficial and genuinely a joy to have in your life. When you find people that you feel good around, positive, and in line with your moral code and standards, you will immediately feel the difference in your life. These are the people who bring out the best in you. This includes characteristics or skills that may lie dormant otherwise. Two parts working together and producing something that neither one would achieve on its own is the principle of synergy.

Section 3: Mentoring

The fact that you are reading this book right now proves that you have the capability of being a mentor to someone. Not everyone can read. We all have something we can teach others. Your age, occupation, education, or any other label you may have does not matter. You are still older or more capable than someone at something. We have all learned from other people in our lives, and we owe it to others to be there for them. If you don't feel a moral obligation to help, then there are still good reasons to do it, even for you. You have probably heard of a runner's high, but have you heard of a helper's high? There has been scientific evidence showing that the simple act of helping others leads to a very similar physiological reaction as that of the runner's high.[24]

Mentoring others also reinforces the knowledge in our own minds. It increases our ability to communicate effectively and be an overall, more compassionate person. It also allows us to see a subject from a brand-new perspective, and we will be learning something in the process too.

The act of mentoring brings many benefits to us, but none of these compare to the huge external factor. We don't know everything that goes on in the minds of other people. We don't know the extent of what they need. The very thing they may need most in the world is for someone to take an interest in them and to be there for them. Our impact could be much more significant than we think, and we may not ever discover what it did for someone else, but that's okay. It is ultimately for them, not for us.

BAD HABITS

For some of us, we are also much more likely to make justifications after we do something that breaks a streak the second time we feel tempted. If we gave in and ate ice cream despite being on a diet, the next sweet that comes in front of us that day will have a higher tendency of going down our bellies. We can justify this by saying that we already messed up, so we might as well just start over tomorrow. I have been guilty of this myself, but this is a horrible philosophy to live by. In one of my favorite books, Meditations by Marcus Aurelius, he teaches the philosophy of living every moment like it's your last.[25] When we implement this idea into how to think, over time, it will have a huge compounding effect from the outcome of the small actions we take every day.

CONCLUSION

Most of us have admirable goals in our lives, though many do not know where to start in reaching them. It is a strange and chaotic world we live in with so many paths to choose from. There are more opportunities now than ever to create the life you want and achieve greatness. Understanding your values and choosing goals accordingly are the fundamental keys to your success. Setting a solid foundation in the 7 facets of your life will create sustainability in whatever venture you decide to pursue.

Writing this book has been a goal of mine for some time now, and the process has helped me discover and solidify many principles in my own life. My "why" is not done once I have published this book, however. Once this book has helped readers in their own lives, my "why" will be complete. My strong desire to positively impact lives is what has fueled me through this process.

Merely learning the principles in this book without taking action leaves you no better off than before you read this book. Because my goal is to help as many people as possible by giving them the information they need to become happier, more successful, and more giving people, I want you to take action.

1. Pick a goal
2. Figure out your "why"
3. Visualize it
4. Craft your environment

5. Eliminate distractions
6. Make a mind map
7. Decide how to accomplish it
8. Break down your plan into mini-goals
9. Complete the mini-goals

Daily actions

- Visualize end result
- Work on your mini-goals at least 2% of the day (30 mins)
- Give yourself a small reward to positively reinforce your work

Weekly actions

- Quickly review mini-goals to decide if you are on track
- Visualize end result

About The Author

Traveling the world and living in many countries blessed Nathan with the opportunity to befriend several successful people from all walks of life. From these remarkable people, he has learned priceless lessons not skewed by a singular view on the world, that he shares with his readers through his website and this book.

Learn more about Nathan's company Reach Fuel Potential reachfuelpotential.com

If you haven't already, make sure download your free goal setting template at reachfuelpotential.com/359-2/

Follow Nathan on Pinterest at pinterest.com/reachfuelpotential/

One Last Thing...

Thank you for taking the time to read my book! If you enjoyed it or found it useful, I'd be very grateful if you'd post a short review on Amazon. A lot of time went into this, but if I make a difference in one person's life, then it will have been worth it to me. Your support really does make a difference, and I read all the reviews personally to get your feedback and make this book even better. I want to improve the lives of as many people as I can, and with your support and feedback, I can impact more people.

Thank you!

-Nathan

Notes

Chapter 1

1.   Bryant, J. (2005). 3:59.4 - The Quest To Break The Four Minute Mile. Arrow Books Ltd.

Chapter 2

1.   Gilovich, T., Medvec, V. H., & Savitsky, K. (2000). The spotlight effect in social judgment: An egocentric bias in estimates of the salience of one's own actions and appearance. Journal of Personality and Social Psychology, 78(2), 211–222. https://doi.org/10.1037/0022-3514.78.2.211

2.   Brown, E. B. (2016). Standing up when life falls down around you (p. 103). United States: Baker Publishing Group.

3.   50 years off-grid: Architect-maker paradise amid NorCal redwoods. (2020, April 26). Retrieved September 19, 2020, from https://www.youtube.com/watch?reload=9

4.   Vaden, R. (2015). Procrastinate on purpose: 5 permissions to multiply your time. New York, NY: Perigee Book.

Chapter 3

5.   [Interview by B. McKenzie]. (1983, January).

6.   Robbins, M. (n.d.). The 5 Second Rule: Transform Your Life, Work, and Confidence with Everyday Courage. United States: Permuted Press.

Chapter 4

1.   Quotes of Michelangelo. (n.d.). Retrieved September 19, 2020, from https://www.michelangelo.org/michelangelo-quotes.jsp

2.   Méndez, M. (2010). METAMORFOSIS DE LA LECTURA. ROMÁN GUBERN. Retrieved September 19, 2020, from https://www.academia.edu/15439709/METAMORFOSIS_DE_LA_LECTURA_ROM%C3%81N_GUBERN

3.   Milutinović, V. (2017). *DataFlow supercomputing essentials: Research, development and education* (p. 136). Cham: Springer.

4.   TheGuitarLesson.com, T. (2020, July 26). How Long Does it Take to Learn Guitar? Retrieved September 19, 2020, from https://www.theguitarlesson.com/guitar-lesson-blog/guitar-lessons/how-long-does-it-take-to-learn-guitar/

Chapter 5

1.   Mihaly Csikszentmihalyi. (2009). *Flow: the psychology of optimal experience* (p. 3). New York: Harper [And] Row.

2.   Collins, B. (2020, March 3). The Pomodoro Technique Explained. Retrieved September 19, 2020, from Forbes website:

https://www.forbes.com/sites/bryancollinseurope/2020/03/03/
the-pomodoro-technique/#3597d0d83985

3.   Newport, C. (2016). *Deep work*. London: Piatkus.

4.   Marta Mestrovic Deyrup. (2018). *Librarian's guide to
writing for professional publication* (p. 31). Santa Barbara,
California: Libraries Unlimited.

5.   What you need to know about willpower: The
psychological science of self-control.
(2012). *Https://Www.Apa.Org*. Retrieved from
https://www.apa.org/topics/willpower

6.   Gailliot, M. T., & Baumeister, R. F. (2007). The
Physiology of Willpower: Linking Blood Glucose to Self-Control.
Personality and Social Psychology Review, 11(4), 303–327.
https://doi.org/10.1177/1088868307303030

7.   #52 Hack Away the Unessentials. (n.d.). Retrieved
September 19, 2020, from Bruce Lee website:
https://brucelee.com/podcast-blog/2017/6/28/52-hack-away-
the-unessentials

8.   Duignan, B. (2018). Occam's razor | Origin, Examples, &
Facts. In *Encyclopædia Britannica*. Retrieved from
https://www.britannica.com/topic/Occams-razor

9.   Shaw, I., & Holland, S. (2014). *Doing qualitative research
in social work* (p. 200). London: Sage.

10.   Knight, C., & Haslam, S. A. (2010). The relative merits of
lean, enriched, and empowered offices: an experimental
examination of the impact of workspace management

strategies on well-being and productivity. *Journal of experimental psychology. Applied, 16*(2), 158–172. https://doi.org/10.1037/a0019292

11.   Agarwal, Dr. P. (2018, December 31). How Does Lighting Affect Mental Health In The Workplace. Retrieved September 19, 2020, from Forbes website: https://www.forbes.com/sites/pragyaagarwaleurope/2018/12/31/how-does-lighting-affect-mental-health-in-the-workplace/#688979584ccd

12.   University of Exeter. (2014, September 1). University of Exeter. Retrieved September 19, 2020, from www.exeter.ac.uk website: http://www.exeter.ac.uk/news/featurednews/title_409094_en.html

13.   Bhasin, M. K., Denninger, J. W., Huffman, J. C., Joseph, M. G., Niles, H., Chad-Friedman, E., … Libermann, T. A. (2018). Specific Transcriptome Changes Associated with Blood Pressure Reduction in Hypertensive Patients After Relaxation Response Training. *The Journal of Alternative and Complementary Medicine, 24*(5), 486–504. https://doi.org/10.1089/acm.2017.0053

14.   Wagner, H. (2006, January 11). Crossing Boundaries: Ohio State Scientist Discusses Stress, Immunity with Dalai Lama. Retrieved September 21, 2020, from Crossing Boundaries: Ohio State Scientist Discusses Stress, Immunity with Dalai Lama website: https://news.osu.edu/crossing-boundaries--ohio-state-scientist-discusses-stress-immunity-with-dalai-lama/

15.   Parvin, P. (2011). Mind Over Matters. *Emory Magazine.* Retrieved from https://www.emory.edu/EMORY_MAGAZINE/issues/2011/wint er/ofnote/meditation/index.html#:~:text=%E2%80%9CData%20 show%20that%20people%20who,principal%20investigator%20o f%20the%20study.&text=%E2%80%9CMeditation%20is%20not %20just%20about%20sitting%20quietly%2C%E2%80%9D%20sa ys%20Negi.

16.   Lamothe, C. (2019, October 3). Decision Fatigue: What It Is and How to Avoid It. Retrieved September 21, 2020, from Healthline website: https://www.healthline.com/health/decision-fatigue#how-it-works

17.   Klein, H. J., Lount, R. B., Park, H. M., & Linford, B. J. (2020). When goals are known: The effects of audience relative status on goal commitment and performance. *Journal of Applied Psychology, 105*(4), 372–389. https://doi.org/10.1037/apl0000441

18.   Gollwitzer, P. M., Sheeran, P., Michalski, V., & Seifert, A. E. (2009). When intentions go public: does social reality widen the intention-behavior gap?. *Psychological science, 20*(5), 612– 618. https://doi.org/10.1111/j.1467-9280.2009.02336.x

19.   Ranganathan, V. K., Siemionow, V., Liu, J. Z., Sahgal, V., & Yue, G. H. (2004). From mental power to muscle power--gaining strength by using the mind. *Neuropsychologia, 42*(7), 944–956. https://doi.org/10.1016/j.neuropsychologia.2003.11.018

20.   Stryker, Dr. L. (n.d.). Emeritus College Journal - ASU. Retrieved September 21, 2020, from emerituscollege.asu.edu website: https://emerituscollege.asu.edu/sites/default/files/ecdw/EVoice10/meditationandmind.html

21.   Quotes of Michelangelo. (n.d.). Retrieved September 19, 2020, from https://www.michelangelo.org/michelangelo-quotes.jsp

7 Facets

1.   D Michael Abrashoff. (2012). It's your ship⬚: management techniques from the best damn ship in the Navy (p. 8). New York: Grand Central Publishing.

2.   D Michael Abrashoff. (2012). It's your ship⬚: management techniques from the best damn ship in the Navy [Audiobook] (1:02:53). New York: Grand Central Publishing.

3.   Ramsey, D. (2018). How It Feels To Have An Emergency Fund - Dave Ramsey Rant [YouTube Video]. Retrieved from https://www.youtube.com/watch?v=n93K_emXggo&feature=youtu.be

4.   Federal Reserve Bank of St. Louis, & Federal Financial Institutions Examination Council (US). (1984, January 1). Return on Average Equity for all U.S. Banks. Retrieved September 21, 2020, from FRED, Federal Reserve Bank of St. Louis website: https://fred.stlouisfed.org/series/USROE

5.   Corley, T. C. (2010). *Rich Habits: The Daily Success Habits of Wealthy Individuals*. Itasca Books.

6.   WebMD. (2008, July 24). Vitamins and Minerals: How Much Should You Take? Retrieved from WebMD website: https://www.webmd.com/vitamins-and-supplements/vitamins-minerals-how-much-should-you-take#1

7.   Oaklander, M. (2016, September 12). The New Science of Exercise. *Time*. Retrieved from https://time.com/4475628/the-new-science-of-exercise/

8.   Saucedo Marquez, C. M., Vanaudenaerde, B., Troosters, T., & Wenderoth, N. (2015). High-intensity interval training evokes larger serum BDNF levels compared with intense continuous exercise. *Journal of Applied Physiology, 119*(12), 1363–1373. https://doi.org/10.1152/japplphysiol.00126.2015

9.   Alexander, A., & Vantine, J. (2015). *Sugar smart express⃞: the 21-day quick start plan to stop cravings, lose weight, and still enjoy the sweets you love!* (p. 251). New York, NY: Rodale.

10.   Schmolesky, M. T., Webb, D. L., & Hansen, R. A. (2013). The Effects of Aerobic Exercise Intensity and Duration on Levels of Brain-Derived Neurotrophic Factor in Healthy Men. *Journal of Sports Science & Medicine, 12*(3), 502–511.

11.   Villines, Z. (2017, October 12). Drinking hot water: Benefits and risks. Retrieved September 22, 2020, from www.medicalnewstoday.com website: https://www.medicalnewstoday.com/articles/319673#benefits-of-drinking-hot-water

12.   Boschmann, M., Steiniger, J., Hille, U., Tank, J., Adams, F., Sharma, A. M., Klaus, S., Luft, F. C., & Jordan, J. (2003). Water-induced thermogenesis. *The Journal of clinical endocrinology and metabolism, 88*(12), 6015–6019. https://doi.org/10.1210/jc.2003-030780

13.   Patel, S., Patel, J., Patel, M., & Jyoti Sen, Dr. D. (2015). Say yes to warm for remove harm: Amazing wonders of two stages of water! *EUROPEAN JOURNAL OF PHARMACEUTICAL AND MEDICAL RESEARCH, 2*(4), 444–460. Retrieved from https://storage.googleapis.com/journal-uploads/ejpmr/article_issue/1435658742.pdf

14.   Oppezzo, M., & Schwartz, D. L. (2014). Give your ideas some legs: The positive effect of walking on creative thinking. *Journal of Experimental Psychology: Learning, Memory, and Cognition, 40*(4), 1142–1152. https://doi.org/10.1037/a0036577

15.   Newport, C. (2016b). *Deep Work* (p. 150). London: Piatkus.

16.   Mcgonigal, K. (2013). The Willpower Instinct: How self-control works, why it matters, and what you can do to get more of it. New York: Avery.

17.   ThoughtTechnologyLtd. (2014). HRV Training and its Importance - Richard Gevirtz, Ph.D., Pioneer in HRV Research & Training [YouTube Video]. Retrieved from https://www.youtube.com/watch?v=9nwFUKuJSE0

18.   Tseng, J., Poppenk, J. Brain meta-state transitions demarcate thoughts across task contexts exposing the mental noise of trait neuroticism. *Nat Commun* **11,** 3480 (2020). https://doi.org/10.1038/s41467-020-17255-9

19.   Holt-Lunstad, J., Smith, T. B., & Layton, J. B. (2010). Social Relationships and Mortality Risk: A Meta-analytic Review. *PLoS Medicine, 7*(7), e1000316. https://doi.org/10.1371/journal.pmed.1000316

20.   Maher, B. (2007). *When you ride alone you still ride with bin Laden⍰: what the government should be telling us to help fight the War on Terrorism.* Beverly Hills, Calif.: Phoenix Books.

21.   TEDx Talks. (2015). Why I read a book a day (and why you should too): the law of 33% | Tai Lopez | TEDxUBIWiltz [YouTube Video]. Retrieved from https://www.youtube.com/watch?v=7bB_fVDlvhc

22.   Social Studies Lessons for Elementary Students. (n.d.). Retrieved October 7, 2020, from Mind Missions website: https://mindmissions.com/social-studies-lessons-framework/discover-elementary-social-studies-lessons/

23.   Collins, J. (2003, July 21). Jim Collins - Articles - The 10 Greatest CEOs of All Time. Retrieved October 8, 2020, from www.jimcollins.com website:

https://www.jimcollins.com/article_topics/articles/10-greatest.html

24.   December 2015, J. S. 01. (2015, December 1). The Science Behind the Power of Giving (Op-Ed). Retrieved October 8, 2020, from livescience.com website: https://www.livescience.com/52936-need-to-give-boosted-by-brain-science-and-evolution.html

25.   Aurelius, M. (2019b). Meditations. Independently published.

Made in the USA
Coppell, TX
07 December 2020

43597936R00066